A JOYFUL
MOTHER
of CHILDREN

A JOYFUL
MOTHER
of CHILDREN

A COMPILATION OF PRAYERS, SUGGESTIONS, AND LAWS FOR THE JEWISH EXPECTANT FAMILY

By
Rabbi Dovid Simcha Rosenthal

FIRST EDITION
First Impression . . . . February, 1982
SECOND EDITION
Revised and Corrected
First Impression . . . . June, 1988
Copyright © 1982, 1988
by
Rabbi Dovid Simcha Rosenthal
1424 Avenue R
Brooklyn, New York 11229
(718) 336–7155

Sole Trade Distribution:

PHILIPP FELDHEIM Inc.
200 Airport Executive Park
Spring Valley, N.Y. 10977

FELDHEIM PUBLISHERS Ltd.
POB 6525 / Jerusalem, Israel

Library of Congress Catalog Card No. 88–091196

ISBN 0-87306-978-1 (hardcover)
ISBN 0-87306-979-X (paperback)

Typography by
Simcha Graphic Associates
4914 13th Avenue
Brooklyn, New York 11219

Printed in the United States of America
Moriah Offset
115 Empire Blvd. ● B'klyn, NY ● 718-693-3800

כל שרוח הבריות נוחה הימנו
רוח המקום נוחה הימנו

מוקדש

לזכר נשמת אבי מורי

ר׳ שמואל בן ר׳ ניסן ע״ה

נפטר י״ב שבט תשמ״ז

ת נ צ ב ה

* * * * * *

Dedicated in Everlasting Memory
Of My Beloved Father
Samuel Rosenthal ע״ה

May His Good Name and Righteous
Deeds Live on Forever

RABBI MOSES FEINSTEIN

455 F. D. R. DRIVE

New York, N. Y. 10002

—

ORegon 7-1222

משה פיינשטיין

ר"מ תפארת ירושלים

בנוא יארק

בע"ח

הנה הרה"ג מוהר"ר דוד רוזנטל שליט"א חיבר קונטרוס קצר שבו ליקט
ואסף והסביר כל מיני תפלות והלכות שנוגעות להריון ולידה. והנה
נכדי, שקרא הספר, שבעיקר נכתב באנגלית, שיבחו, וגם שאל ממני בשביל
הרב הנ"ל כמה שאלות, ועל כן הריני מברכו שיצליחהו השי"ת בהדפסת
ספר זה, ויזכה להגדיל תורה ולהאדירה, ובזכות הפרצת התורה נזכה
בקרוב לביאת הגואל.

ועל זה באתי על החתום לכבוד התורה ביום י"ד לחודש כסלו תשמ"ב.

משה פיינשטיין

משה פיינשטיין

ב"ה

𝕸𝖎𝖗𝖗𝖊𝖗 𝖄𝖊𝖘𝖍𝖎𝖛𝖆

BETH MEDRASH
POST GRADUATE SCHOOL
KOLEL

𝕮𝖊𝖓𝖙𝖗𝖆𝖑 𝕴𝖓𝖘𝖙𝖎𝖙𝖚𝖙𝖊

HIGH SCHOOL
SEPHARDIC DIVISION
TEACHERS INSTITUTE

GEN. ADMINISTRATIVE OFFICE: 1791-5 OCEAN PARKWAY BROOKLYN, N. Y. 11223
NI 5-0536-7

RABBI SHRAGE MOSHE KALMANOWITZ
RABBI SHMUEL BERENBAUM
Roshei Yeshiva

מיסדו של
מרן הגאון
ר' אברהם קלמנוביץ זצ"ל

Founded by
RABBI ABRAHAM KALMANOWITZ זצ"ל

ידידי הנעלה הרב הגאון המצוין הרב ר' דוד רוזנטל, שליט"א
שלמד בישיבתינו מטל ילדותו עד היום הזה ועלה ונתעלה בתורה
ויראת שמים כפי כשרונותיו הנעלים.

רחש לבו דבר טוב להוציא לאור קונטריסים שיש בהם
תפילות מלוקטים מדברי רבותינו הקדמונים ז"ל בשביל תקופות
שונות של ימי העבור.   וגם תפילות וברכות שנוגעות לזמן
הלידה.   עצם הליקוט הנ"ל יש בזה זיכוי הרבים בכמה מובנים.
ראשית דבר עצם הידעות הנחוצות שמביא, וגם התעוררות שבא לאדם
מזה שצריכים רחמי שמים וחסדי השי"ת על כל צעד וצעד ובשביל כל
מצב ומצב המתרחש בחיי האדם.   וגם מדיני הברכות בשביל זמן
הלידה והאדם מתעורר להכיר חסדי השם המקיפים אותו מכל צד כל
ימי חייו, מצוה גוררת מצוה.   ויהי רצון שיזכה לזכות את
הרבים כל ימי חייו, ומגלגלים זכות ע'י זכאי,

שרגא משה קלמנוביץ   יום ב'   ט' טבת תשמ"ב

Mirrer Yeshiva

Central Institute

BETH MEDRASH
POST GRADUATE SCHOOL
KOLEL

HIGH SCHOOL
SEPHARDIC DIVISION
TEACHERS INSTITUTE

GEN. ADMINISTRATIVE OFFICE: 1791-5 OCEAN PARKWAY   BROOKLYN, N. Y. 11223

RABBI SHRAGE MOSHE KALMANOWITZ
RABBI SHMUEL BERENBAUM
Roshei Yeshiva

NI 5-0536-7

מיסודו של
מרן הגאון
ר' אברהם קלמנוביץ זצ"ל

Founded by
RABBI ABRAHAM KALMANOWITZ תי"ל

אור ליום ג' צום העשירי יהפך לששון ושמחה במהרה בימינו, תשמ"ב

הנה מע"כ ידידי היקר עדין הנפש ובעל המעשים, הרב הגאון
ר' דוד רוזנסל שליט"א, רחש לבו דבר טוב בעתו להוציא לאור קונטרס
תפילות הלכות וסגולות הנוגעים לתקופת ההריון והלידה. והנה מלבד
התועלת הרבה בזכוי הרבים לסייעתא דשמיא בכח התפילות וכו', ובפרט
בדבר שהוא מג' המפתחות שלא נמסרו ע"י שליח, עוד הגדיל לעשות להשריש
בלב האדם את האמונה הטהורה כי כל דברינו מקרינו כולם ניסים אין בהם טבע
ומנהגו של עולם כדברי הרמב"ן סוף פ' בא, וכי אנו גוי גדול אשר לו אלקים
קרובים אליו בכל קראנו אליו. וכהיותי עד לעמל הרב שהשקיע המחבר
להוציא לאור דבר לאשורו. אמינא לפעלו טבא וישר חילה לזכות את
הרבים תמיד כיקרת נפשו הטהורה. ובזכות האמונה נזכה במהרה לגאולה
ולקיום המפתח השלישי, כמבואר במדרש תנחומא פ' בשלח ואין הגלויות
עתידות להגאל אלא בשכר האמונה אכי"ר.

בחותם באהבה,
דן זאב הלוי סגל

Rabbi **CHAIM P. SCHEINBERG**

KIRYAT MATTERSDORF
PANIM MEIROT 2
JERUSALEM, ISRAEL

הרב חיים פנחס שיינברג
ראש ישיבת "תורה אור"
ומורה הוראה דקרית מטרסדורף
ירושלים טל.911912

בס"ד

הנה בא אלי מכרי משנים רבות, האברך היקר
הרה"ג מוהר"ר ר' דוד שמחה רוזנטל שליט"א, מחשובי תלמידי
בישיבתינו הקדושה בירדושלים עה"ק מלפנים, אתא ואייתי
מתניתי' בידי' מהדורה מתוקנת מספרו "אם הבנים שמחה",
מכיל הרבה דינים נחוצים לעוברות, יולדות, ומניקות,
כגון דיני שבת ויום הכפורים, נדה, תענית, ברכות הודאה
וכו' הנוגעים להן, גם סגולות ותפלות מלוקטות מספרים
קדושים להתפלל לפני הלידה. וכל זה מתורגם לשפה המדוברת
כדי לאפשר לאלה שאינן רגילות בלשון הקדש להבין אותו.
ואמינא לפעלא טבא יישר כי זה דבר מועיל מאד. והנני
מברכו בהצלחה רבה.

ועל זה באתי על החתום לכבוד התורה ולומדי'
ביום ה' לסדר זאת תורת היולדת
ד' אייר שנת תשמ"ח לפ"ק י'ם למב"י.

חיים פנחס שיינברג

RABBI YISROEL P. GORNISH
1421 Avenue O
Brooklyn, N.Y. 11230
(718) 376-3755

ישראל פינחס הלוי גארניש
רב דקהל חיזוק חדת
ברוקלין, נ.י.

בס"ד

מע"כ ידידי הרה"ג ר׳ דוד שמחה רוזנטל שליט"א,
כבר הוציא ספרו "אם הבנים שמחה" הכולל תפלות סגולות
והלכות הנוגעים לזמני הריון ולידה, ומאוד זיכה את
הרבים בו.

מכיון שספרו היקר כמעט אינו בנמצא עוד אצל
מוכרי ספרים רחש לבו דבר טוב להוציאו עוד הפעם עם
הרבה תוספות הלכות הנוגעות למעשה לתקופות ההריון
ועד לאחר הלידה.

בנוגע הלכות אלו הסתופף אצלי פעמים הרבה כדי
לברר ההלכות על בוריס ושיהיו ברורים ונקיים מכל טעות,
ח"ו לכל הקורא אותם.

ברכתי שיראה המחבר הצלחה בהרבצת התורה ושזכות
הרבים תעמוד לו ולבני ביתו ושזכות התורה יעמוד לנו
ולכל ישראל בבג"א.

יא סיון תשמ"ח

ישראל פינחס הלוי גארניש

TABLE OF CONTENTS

PREFACE

On November 20, 1979 (*Rosh Chodesh Kislev,* 5740) God blessed our family with a third child. I remember well the pain my wife endured at that time, and during the deliveries of my other two children.

‏„אין אדם נוקף אצבעו מלמטה אלא אם כן מכריזין עליו מלמעלה.‟ (חולין ז:)

"No man injures his finger on earth unless there is a heavenly decree." (*Chulin* 7b)

Chazal (our sages) tell us that even insignificant events do not occur without the involvement of God. Every slightest action is under His supervision. If a person wanted to take three coins out of his pocket, and he took out only two, this would be considered suffering (*Erechin* 16b).

Our sages tell us (*Brochos* 8a) that the formula to be followed when troubles come, is to examine one's deeds and do *teshuva* (repent). They give us other options as well; such as prayer— ‏„תפילה מגינה על הצרה כצינה שמגינה על האדם במלחמה.‟ (אסתר רבה י:ט) "Prayer protects us from trouble as a shield protects a man at war." (*Esther Raba* 10:9)

‏„אפילו חרב חדה מונחת לו על צוארו של אדם, אל ימנע עצמו מן הרחמים.‟ (ברכות י.) "Even if a sharp sword is (already) placed on a man's neck, he should not cease to plead for mercy." (*Brochos* 10a)

In *Eruvin* 100b, *Chazal* describe what is written in Genesis 3:16, regarding the woman's punishment in all generations because of the sin of *Chava*: She will encounter discomfort during the course of her pregnancy, and she will undergo great pain during labor and delivery.

Our first two children were born with great pain, and before the third delivery, we felt we needed to put in more effort to make this one easier. I became aware that there are various prayers that can be said for such a time. Thank God, the labor and delivery of our third child was much easier, (*She'lo ke'derech ha-teva* שלא כדרך הטבע). What helped? Only God knows.

My wife's obstetrician took me home from the hospital that day. In the car (and even earlier that day, in the hospital) I thought about what had happened. I said to the doctor, "Do you think it would be a good idea to print up some of these prayers in one work to make them more readily available when necessary? He seemed to think it would be a good idea. This discussion was the first thought in compiling this book. I hope that this work, *A Joyful Mother of Children,* will help those in similar circumstances to make use of the material that was written by our early sages, and result with God's help in an easier pregnancy, labor and delivery.

The reader should note that a glossary has been included, translating all the italicized Hebrew terms. A bibliography with biographical information about the authors and works cited has also been provided.

ACKNOWLEDGEMENTS
FIRST EDITION

I wish to thank *Ha-Kadosh Boruch Hu* for giving me the opportunity to study His *Torah,* and for leading me in His ways. I thank Him for enabling me to accomplish this task, and I hope that this work will aid many Jewish mothers during their moments of travail.

I am deeply indebted to the Mirrer Yeshiva where I have been privileged to learn for more than half of my life. The *Roshei HaYeshiva* and the *Rabbeim* have been instrumental in instilling in me love for *Hashem's Torah* and *mitzvos.* May they have continued success in spreading the *Torah* of *Hashem.*

Several of our great Rabbis and *halachic* authorities have helped me in the writing and publishing of this *sefer.* I would like to thank *Harav Hagaon* Rabbi Moshe Feinstein, שליט"א, who spent some of his most precious time in giving me his *halachic* decisions.

I would like to thank Rabbi Mordechai Tendler and Rabbi Laibel Berenbaum for reading through the manuscript. I appreciate their interest and their suggestions.

A deeply felt *HaKoras Ha-tov* goes to *Harav Hagaon* Rabbi Dann Segal, שליט"א the *Mashgiach Ruchani* of Mirrer Yeshiva, whom I consulted frequently throughout my work on the Hebrew text. He generously and selflessly gave of his time.

My sincere appreciation to Rabbi Yaakov Dardac and Rebetzin Yehudis Hager for their professional help with the Hebrew *nikud.* The work they did was invaluable. May *Ha-Kadosh Boruch Hu* repay their kindness.

In addition, I would like to thank the following people who have assisted me in the many facets of this work:

Rabbi Shimon Newhouse for lending me some of the material that was needed; Rabbi Levi Hettleman for helping me gather information; Miss Faigie Zylberminc of the Library of Congress, who so willingly used the resources of her office to provide information; Mrs. Bracha Sacks for her professional editing; Rabbi Shmuel Kunda for the artistic cover design; and Mr. Walter Kairy for his time spent on behalf of this *sefer*.

My sincere appreciation to Yitzchok Feldheim of Feldheim Publishers for his time and valuable suggestions, which are incorporated in this work.

My thanks go to Simcha Graphic Associates for their time and patience in skillfully typesetting this complex work.

A note of extreme gratitude goes to my friend and silent partner, Dr. Sol Neuhoff. He has been interested and involved in the writing and publishing of this text from beginning to end.

I feel a tremendous amount of gratefulness to my father and my mother, Mr. and Mrs. Samuel Rosenthal, for all they have sacrificed selflessly throughout my life, and for giving me the opportunity to learn *Torah*. Also, my heartfelt appreciation goes to my father-in-law and mother-in-law, Mr. and Mrs. Leon Faigenbam, for their deep concern and devotion to my family and me. May *Ha-Kadosh Boruch Hu* grant my parents and my parents-in-law many, many happy years of good health and much *Yiddishe nachas* from all their children and grandchildren.

To my devoted wife Yaffa, שתחי׳, I feel an immeasureable amount of sincere gratitude for enabling me to continue to study *Torah*. She has also been instrumental throughout this project, and without her help, it could not have been completed. May she truly be an אם הבנים שמחה, and together we should be *zocheh* to bring up children and grandchildren בנים ובני בנים עוסקים בתורה ובמצות.

Dovid Simcha Rosenthal
Chanukah 5742

ACKNOWLEDGEMENTS
REVISED EDITION

I wish to express once again my gratitude to *Ha-Kadosh Boruch Hu* for giving me the opportunity to study his *Torah* and enabling me to revise the volume of אם הבנים שמחה/*A Joyful Mother of Children.*

My sincere thanks to those who helped me compile my first volume. Without them, the following would not be possible.

This revised and corrected work is not completely my own. Without the assistance, guidance, direction, counsel and encouragement of Harav Hagaon Rabbi Yisroel Pinchas Gornish שליטא—*Rav* B'Kehal Chizuk Hadas, Brooklyn, N.Y., these additions would not have been possible. I am most grateful for his generosity in giving me of his time and for his patience in helping me. He is actually my co-author on all the additions in the section on *Halacha*. May Rabbi Gornish together with his Rebitzen be *zocheh* to בנים ובני בנים עוסקים בתורה ובמצות.

I am especially grateful to Harav Avrohom Yosef Rosenberg for his much needed talents. His editing skills were applied to the correction of the entire work. He has helped to insure accuracy and correct *nikud* in both the Hebrew and Yiddish texts. Many of his valuable suggestions are incorporated into the final text.

I am indeed grateful to the following people for their precious help:

Rabbi Meshulam Greenfield of Ateres Bookbinding Co. who has granted me permission to re-typeset the *Yiddish Tefillos* which appear in *Techina Kol Bo Ha Chodosh*; my good friend Rabbi Sheah Brander of Mesorah Publications who has helped to redesign the cover in a way that enhanced its original beauty; my long term friend, Dr. Sol Neuhoff for his continual involvement in the publishing of this work.

I would also like to humbly express my sincere thanks to the staff of Simcha Graphic Associates. Their co-operation and patience combined with their expert typesetting ability has been instrumental in obtaining a nearly error-free and high level graphic publication.

A loving sense of gratitude to my dear mother, Mrs. Miriam Rosenthal שתחי׳. She has not only helped me in this undertaking but has sacrificed much to insure that my family and I follow the Torah path. Also, to my father-in-law and mother-in-law, Mr. and Mrs. Leon Faigenbam, I would like to express grateful appreciation for their continuous selflessness and caring for my family and me. May *Ha-Kadosh Boruch Hu* grant my mother and parents-in-law generations of *Yiddishe nachas* and good health.

A heartful feeling of deep sincere gratitude to my faithful and caring wife מנשים באהל תברך, Yaffa שתחי׳. I am truly thankful to her for her encouragement to continue the study of *Torah* and making the completion of this work possible. May she indeed be an אם הבנים שמחה in good health עמו״ש. And together we should be *zocheh* to our mutual desire of לא ימושו מפיך ומפי זרעך ומפי זרע זרעך אמר ה׳ מעתה ועד עולם.

Dovid Simcha Rosenthal
13 Sivan 5748

INTRODUCTION

„לעולם יבקש אדם רחמים שלא יחלה שאם יחלה אומרים לו הבא זכות
והפטר." (שבת לב.) "A man should always pray (for mercy), that
he should not become ill; for when one is taken ill he is told,
'Bring evidence in your favor and then you will be acquitted
(from the illness).'" (*Shabbos* 32a)

Chazal tell us that a person should pray to God before
troubles come. They are referring to normal circumstances,
and not, God forbid, to a time of epidemic or widespread
disease. So, even if one does not have any reason to believe he
will become ill, he should turn to God and ask Him to keep
him in good health. If one does enter a situation of possible
danger, *tefillah* (prayer) certainly is of the utmost importance.

The Talmud in Tractate *Berachos* 60a tells us that one
should start to ask for mercy even before conception. In
accordance with this, the *Ramban* has a special *tefillah* (found
in the *Siddur* of *Rav* Yaakov Emden, סידור בית יעקב בסדר ליל
שבת) to be said before conception.

Pregnancy is certainly an important time for one to ask
God for mercy. One should beseech God that everything
should be successful.

„וכל מאמינים שהוא יוצרם בבטן", It is God who creates us, so it
is to Him we *daven* for everything. ויהי רצון שימלא ה' את כל משאלות
לבנו לטובה. May it be His Will to fulfill all our desires for
the best.

In the following pages you will find listed several prayers
found in religious books, to be said at various times during

23

pregnancy.* Besides these *tefillos* one may and should pray to God by using his own choice of words at any time. Also included are a number of *segulos* (spiritual remedies) and advice found in holy books. At the end of this work are *halachos* that are applicable to the Jewish expectant family. These laws include topics on *Shabbos, niddah,* fasting, impurity of a *Kohen,* blessings to be said after birth, the obligation of the husband to be called up to the *Torah,* and the obligation of saying the Thanksgiving Blessing. The exact wording of the blessings to be said immediately after birth can be found in the Appendix.

* Please note that when a *tefillah* is said for someone, that person's Hebrew name must be recited: so and so, the daughter of so and so, mentioning the mother's name. Also, please note that the English translation of the *tefillos* is not intended to be literal. Rather, it is meant to aid the reader in understanding the meaning of each *tefillah.* In addition, to aid the reader, the Hebrew *tefillos* were vowelized.

תפילות

* * * * * * * *

PRAYERS

To be recited by the husband
when his wife enters
her third month of pregnancy.

(*Taken from the Sefer Avodas Ha-Kodesh.*)

Yours, O God, is the greatness and the power, the glory, the victory and the majesty, for all that is in heaven and on earth is Yours. Yours is the sovereignty, and all that which rules over anything on earth. Master of the universe, with a broken and humble heart, I pray before the throne of Your mercy. Although I know that I am not at all worthy, I have placed Your mercy before me, because You are merciful. Therefore, may it be Your will, O God, and God of our fathers, that You be filled with mercy for the sake of all the pregnant women of Your nation, Israel, and specifically for my wife (the woman's name and mother's name). May You ease the suffering of her pregnancy, and do it for the sake of Your mercy, so that the embryo should remain in good health in all its limbs and blood vessels. All should be well; and may my wife not miscarry, for the sake of Your great mercy, in Your holy name of *אל חד*. May her term of pregnancy be complete, and may she not miscarry, as the earth brings forth its growth and as the seeds of a garden sprout forth, so should be Your will.

---

* The words themselves are not read; rather one should pronounce only the Hebrew letters individually.

aleph,   lamed — ches,   dalet

תפלה לבעל
כשאשתו נכנסת
לחדש השלישי בעיבורה

(לקח מספר עבודת הקודש—סנסן ליאיר)

לְךָ יְיָ הַגְּדֻלָּה וְהַגְּבוּרָה וְהַתִּפְאֶרֶת וְהַגֵּצַח וְהַהוֹד כִּי כֹל בַּשָּׁמַיִם וּבָאָרֶץ לְךָ יְיָ הַמַּמְלָכָה וְהַמִּתְנַשֵּׂא לְכֹל לְרֹאש: רִבּוֹנוֹ שֶׁל-עוֹלָם, בְּלֵב נִשְׁבָּר וְנִדְכֶּה אֲנִי מִתְפַּלֵּל לִפְנֵי כִסֵּא רַחֲמֶיךָ וְהַגַּם שֶׁיָּדַעְתִּי שֶׁאֵינִי כְדַאי כְּלָל שַׁמְתִּי רַחֲמֶיךָ לְנֶגֶד עֵינַי כִּי רַחוּם אַתָּה, וּבְכֵן יְהִי רָצוֹן מִלְּפָנֶיךָ יְיָ אֱלֹהֵינוּ וֵאלֹהֵי אֲבוֹתֵינוּ שֶׁתִּתְמַלֵּא רַחֲמִים עַל כָּל-עֻבָּרוֹת עַמְּךָ יִשְׂרָאֵל וּבִפְרָט עַל אִשְׁתִּי (פְּלוֹנִית בַּת פְּלוֹנִית) וְתָקֵל מֵעָלֶיהָ צַעַר הָעִבּוּר וַעֲשֵׂה לְמַעַן רַחֲמֶיךָ שֶׁיִּתְקַיֵּם הָעֻבָּר בִּבְרִיאוּת וְיִגָּמֵר לְטוֹבָה בְּכָל-אֵבָרָיו וְגִידָיו וְהַכֹּל מְתֻקָּן וְלֹא תַפִּיל אִשְׁתִּי לְמַעַן רַחֲמֶיךָ הַמְרֻבִּים בְּשִׁמְךָ הַקָּדוֹשׁ **אל חד** וְיִמְלְאוּ יָמֶיהָ לָלֶדֶת וְלֹא תִהְיֶה מַשְׁכֵּלָה כִּי כָאָרֶץ תּוֹצִיא צִמְחָהּ וּכְגַנָּה זֵרוּעֶיהָ תַצְמִיחַ, כֵּן יְהִי רָצוֹן.

*לֹא לִקְרֹא אֶת הַמִּלִּים רַק לְבַטֵּא אֶת הָאוֹתִיּוֹת: אָלֶף, לָמֶד — חֵית, דָּלֶת

To be recited by the husband when his wife enters her seventh month of pregnancy.

(*Taken from the Sefer Kitzur Sh'nei Luchos Ha-Bris.*)

May it be Your will, O God, and God of our fathers, that You relieve my wife's (the woman's name and mother's name) suffering during her pregnancy, and continue to give her strength for her entire pregnancy, so that her strength and the strength of the fetus should not wane in any manner. May You save her from the fate of Chava. May it be at the time that she is ready to give birth, when her term of pregnancy is complete, that her labor pains should not be unduly oppressive, and the child should be born into the world without delay. May she have an easy delivery without any damage to her or to the child. May the child be born at an opportune time with good fortune. May he have a good life with peace and good health, with favor and kindness, with wealth and honor. [May my wife not give birth on Shabbos so that it should not be necessary to profane the Shabbos, God forbid, because of her.] May You fulfill all my requests in good measure, with salvation and compassion in the midst of all Israel that are in need of mercy. Please do not turn me away empty-handed from before You.

תפלה לבעל
כשאשתו נכנסת
לחדש השביעי בעיבורה
(לקח מספר קיצור שני לוחות הברית)

יְהִי רָצוֹן מִלְּפָנֶיךָ יי אֱלֹהֵינוּ וֵאלֹהֵי אֲבוֹתֵינוּ שֶׁתָּקֵל מֵעַל אִשְׁתִּי מָרַת (פְּלוֹנִית בַּת פְּלוֹנִית) אֶת צַעַר עֲבוּרָהּ וְתוֹסִיף וְתִתֶּן לָהּ כֹּחַ כָּל-יְמֵי הָעִבּוּר שֶׁלֹּא יֶתַּשׁ כֹּחָהּ וְלֹא כֹחַ הָעֻבָּר בְּשׁוּם דָּבָר בָּעוֹלָם וְתַצִּיל אוֹתָהּ מִפִּתְקָהּ שֶׁל חַוָּה וִיהִי בְּעֵת לְדָתָהּ כִּי יִמְלְאוּ יָמֶיהָ לָלֶדֶת, לֹא יֵהָפְכוּ עָלֶיהָ צִירֵי לֵדָה וְיֵצֵא הַנּוֹלָד לַאֲוִיר הָעוֹלָם בְּרֶגַע קָטָן וְתֵלֵד בְּנָקֵל בְּלִי שׁוּם הֶזֵּק לָהּ וְלֹא לַנּוֹלָד וְיִהְא נוֹלָד בְּשָׁעָה טוֹבָה וּמַזָּל טוֹב לְחַיִּים וּלְשָׁלוֹם וְלִבְרִיאוּת, לְחֵן וּלְחֶסֶד לְעֹשֶׁר וְכָבוֹד [וְשֶׁלֹּא תֵלֵד אִשְׁתִּי בְּשַׁבָּת כְּדֵי שֶׁלֹּא יִצְטָרְכוּ לְחַלֵּל שַׁבָּת, חַס וְשָׁלוֹם, בִּשְׁבִילָהּ] וּתְמַלֵּא כָּל-מִשְׁאֲלוֹתַי בְּמִדָּה טוֹבָה יְשׁוּעָה וְרַחֲמִים בְּקֶרֶב כָּל-יִשְׂרָאֵל הַצְּרִיכִים רַחֲמִים וְאַל תְּשִׁיבֵנִי רֵיקָם מִלְּפָנֶיךָ אָמֵן.

To be recited by the husband when his wife enters her ninth month of pregnancy.

*(Taken from the Sefer **Kitzur Sh'nei Luchos Ha-Bris.**)*

O merciful One, have mercy on all the daughters of Israel who are giving birth, and among them Your maidservant, my wife (the woman's name and mother's name). We plead to You, merciful and gracious One, for Your mercy is great. In Your hand, O God, is the key, and You did not entrust it to any messenger. Therefore, remember your compassion, O God, and Your kindness, Lord our God, Who desires life. Remember her with salvation and compassion, and may she give birth with relief to abiding offspring worthy of Your holy power. King David, may he rest in peace, the pleasant singer, said, "From the straits I called upon God; He answered me with the generosity of God. God was with me, and I did not fear." (Psalms 118:5) "For the Conductor, a psalm to David. God will answer you in the day of trouble; may the name of the God of Jacob defend you. He will send forth your help from the sanctuary, and will strengthen you from Zion. May He remember all your offerings, and accept with favor your burnt offering. May He grant your heart's desire, and fulfill all your counsel. May we rejoice in Your salvation, and in the name of our God set up our banner. May God fulfill all that you ask. Now I know that God saves His anointed; He answers him from His holy heaven, with the omnipotent acts of salvation of His right hand. Some trust in chariots and some in horses, but as for us, we remember the name of the Lord our God. They are bowed down and fallen, but we have always risen again and have constantly kept ourselves upright. May God grant salvation. The King will answer

תפלה לבעל
כשאשתו נכנסת
לחדש התשיעי בעיבורה

(לקח מספר קיצור שני לוחות הברית)

רַחֲמָנָא רַחֵם עַל יוֹלְדוֹת בְּנוֹת יִשְׂרָאֵל וּבִכְלָלָם אֲמָתְךָ אִשְׁתִּי מָרַת
(פְּלוֹנִית בַּת פְּלוֹנִית) הִנְנוּ מַפִּילִים תַּחֲנוּנֵינוּ לְפָנֶיךָ רַחוּם וְחַנּוּן כִּי
רַבִּים רַחֲמֶיךָ וּבְיָדְךָ יי הַמַּפְתֵּחַ הַזֶּה וְלֹא מְסַרְתּוֹ לְשָׁלִיחַ וּבְכֵן זְכֹר
רַחֲמֶיךָ יי וַחֲסָדֶיךָ יי אֱלֹהֵינוּ הֶחָפֵץ חַיִּים לְפָקְדָהּ בִּישׁוּעָה וְרַחֲמִים
וְתֵלֵד בְּרֶוַח זֶרַע קַיָּמָא וְכָשֵׁר מִסִּטְרָא דְּקַדֻּשָׁה. דָּוִד הַמֶּלֶךְ עָלָיו
הַשָּׁלוֹם, נְעִים זְמִירוֹת, אָמַר: מִן־הַמֵּצַר קָרָאתִי יָהּ עָנָנִי בַמֶּרְחָב יָהּ
יי לִי לֹא אִירָא. לַמְנַצֵּחַ מִזְמוֹר לְדָוִד: יַעַנְךָ יי בְּיוֹם צָרָה, יְשַׂגֶּבְךָ שֵׁם
אֱלֹהֵי יַעֲקֹב: יִשְׁלַח עֶזְרְךָ מִקֹּדֶשׁ, וּמִצִּיּוֹן יִסְעָדֶךָּ: יִזְכֹּר כָּל־מִנְחֹתֶיךָ,
וְעוֹלָתְךָ יְדַשְּׁנֶה סֶלָה: יִתֶּן־לְךָ כִלְבָבֶךָ, וְכָל־עֲצָתְךָ יְמַלֵּא: נְרַנְּנָה
בִּישׁוּעָתֶךָ, וּבְשֵׁם אֱלֹהֵינוּ נִדְגֹּל, יְמַלֵּא יי כָּל מִשְׁאֲלוֹתֶיךָ: עַתָּה
יָדַעְתִּי כִּי הוֹשִׁיעַ יי מְשִׁיחוֹ יַעֲנֵהוּ מִשְּׁמֵי קָדְשׁוֹ, בִּגְבוּרוֹת יֵשַׁע
יְמִינוֹ: אֵלֶּה בָרֶכֶב וְאֵלֶּה בַסּוּסִים וַאֲנַחְנוּ בְּשֵׁם יי אֱלֹהֵינוּ נַזְכִּיר:
הֵמָּה כָּרְעוּ וְנָפָלוּ, וַאֲנַחְנוּ קַמְנוּ וַנִּתְעוֹדָד: יי הוֹשִׁיעָה הַמֶּלֶךְ יַעֲנֵנוּ

us on the day on which we call upon Him." (Psalms 20) He Who heeded the prayers of David, may He heed our prayers in the merit of the patriarchs and matriarchs. He Who answered our holy matriarchs, Sarah, Rebecca, Rachel, Leah and Chana, and all the righteous, pious, and worthy women, may He answer us. May the words of my mouth and the meditation of my heart be pleasing before You, O God, my Rock and my Redeemer.

בְּיוֹם קָרְאֵנוּ: מִי שֶׁשָּׁמַע תְּפִלַּת דָּוִד הוּא יִשְׁמַע תְּפִלָּתֵנוּ בִּזְכוּת
הָאָבוֹת וְהָאִמָּהוֹת, מִי שֶׁעָנָה לְאִמּוֹתֵינוּ הַקְּדוֹשׁוֹת: שָׂרָה רִבְקָה רָחֵל
וְלֵאָה וְחַנָּה וּלְכָל צַדִּיקוֹת וַחֲסִידוֹת וְהַגּוּנוֹת הוּא יַעֲנֵנוּ. יִהְיוּ לְרָצוֹן
אִמְרֵי פִי וְהֶגְיוֹן לִבִּי לְפָנֶיךָ יי צוּרִי וְגוֹאֲלִי.

**To be recited by the husband
when his wife enters her
ninth month of pregnancy.**

(*Taken from the Sefer Avodas Ha-Kodesh.*)

May it be Your will, O God, our God, and God of our
fathers, that You have mercy upon all pregnant women of
Your nation that are giving birth, and specifically upon my
wife (the woman's name and mother's name). At the time that
she is giving birth, may You ease the sufferings of her labor, so
she may give birth easily without any suffering, before any pain
of labor comes upon her. May her child come forth to a good
and peaceful life, at a good time, with good fortune for us and
for the child. May no suffering, damage or misfortune occur,
God forbid, to her or to the child. O God full of mercy, may
Your mercy come forth on behalf of my wife, the aforemen-
tioned, and save her from all pain, disorder, and from confu-
sion. May she deliver the placenta in its proper time, and may
she be healthy and well for Your service. A broken and a
humble heart, O God, You will not despise. In the name of
אראריתא may You heed our prayers, and answer our beseech-
ing. For You are merciful and You hear the prayers of every
mouth. May the words of my mouth and the meditation of my
heart be pleasing before You, O God, my Rock and my
Redeemer.

---

* The word itself is not to be read, rather one should pronounce only the
hebrew letters individually.
aleph, raish, aleph, raish, yud, suv, aleph

תפלה לבעל
כשאשתו נכנסת
לחדש התשיעי בעיבורה

(לקח מספר עבודת הקודש—סנסן ליאיר)

יְהִי רָצוֹן מִלְּפָנֶיךָ יי אֱלֹהֵינוּ וֵאלֹהֵי אֲבוֹתֵינוּ שֶׁתְּרַחֵם עַל־כָּל־
עֻבָּרוֹת הַיוֹלְדוֹת מֵעַמְּךָ יִשְׂרָאֵל וּבִפְרָט עַל אִשְׁתִּי (פְּלוֹנִית בַּת
פְּלוֹנִית) וּבְעֵת לִדְתָּהּ תָּקֵל מֵעָלֶיהָ צַעַר הַלֵּדָה וְתֵלֵד בְּנָקֵל בְּלִי שׁוּם
צַעַר, בְּטֶרֶם יָבֹא חֵבֶל לָהּ וְהִמְלִיטָה עֻבָּרָהּ לְחַיִּים טוֹבִים וּלְשָׁלוֹם
בְּשָׁעָה טוֹבָה וּמַזָּל לָנוּ וְלַוָּלָד, וְלֹא יֶאֱרַע לָהּ וְלֹא לַוָּלָד שׁוּם צַעַר
וְשׁוּם נֶזֶק וְשׁוּם מִקְרֶה רָע חַס וְשָׁלוֹם. אֵל מָלֵא רַחֲמִים יֶהֱמוּ נָא
רַחֲמֶיךָ עַל אִשְׁתִּי הַנִּזְכֶּרֶת וְתַצִּילֶהָ מִכָּל־כְּאֵב וְטֵרוּף וּבֶהָלָה וְתֵצֵא
הַשִּׁלְיָא בִּזְמַנָּהּ וְתִהְיֶה בְּרִיאָה וְטוֹבָה לַעֲבוֹדָתֶךָ. לֵב נִשְׁבָּר וְנִדְכֶּה
אֱלֹהִים לֹא תִבְזֶה וּבְשֵׁם *אראריתא* תִּשְׁמַע תְּפִלָּתֵנוּ וְתַעֲנֶה
עֲתִירָתֵנוּ כִּי רַחוּם אַתָּה וְשׁוֹמֵעַ תְּפִלַּת כָּל־פֶּה. יִהְיוּ לְרָצוֹן אִמְרֵי פִי
וְהֶגְיוֹן לִבִּי לְפָנֶיךָ יי צוּרִי וְגוֹאֲלִי.

---

*לֹא לִקְרֹא אֶת הַמִּלָּה רַק לְבַטֵּא אֶת הָאוֹתִיּוֹת: אָלֶף, רֵישׁ, אָלֶף, רֵישׁ, יוֹד, תָּו, אָלֶף

To be recited by the husband
when his wife is in active labor.*

(Adapted from Sefer Shevet Mussar, Chapter 24.)

May it be Your will, O great, mighty and awesome God, that the merit of this afflicted woman who is trembling and crying out in her pangs of childbirth, be mentioned before You. If she has had any sin, may You forgive and cleanse it through her suffering, the pains of her labor. May the sound of her crying out ascend to Your Throne of Glory. Seal the mouth of her accusers, but may all defenders on her behalf, for good, be gathered before You as Your attribute is to bestow goodness on the worthy and unworthy alike. May Your mercy spread upon her, for You are He Who answers in time of distress, O Compassionate King who is merciful to all, Who redeems and saves, hears and answers.

* **Please Note:** If one finds himself in a hospital room that has a cross on the wall and it cannot be removed or covered up, then he should *daven* not facing the cross.

תפלה
כשהאשה יושבת על המשבר

(על פי ספר שבט מוסר פרק כ"ד)

יְהִי רָצוֹן מִלְּפָנֶיךָ הַשֵּׁם הַגָּדוֹל הַגִּבּוֹר וְהַנּוֹרָא שֶׁיַּזְכִּירוּ לְפָנֶיךָ זְכוּת הָאִשָּׁה הָעֲנִיָּה הַזֹּאת אֲשֶׁר תָּחִיל וְתִזְעַק בַּחֲבָלֶיהָ, וְאִם יֵשׁ בָּהּ שׁוּם עָוֹן, מְחֹל וּמְרֹק אוֹתוֹ בַּמֶּה שֶׁנִּצְטַעֲרָה בִּכְאֵב הַחֲבָלִים וְתַעֲלֶה קוֹל צַעֲקָתָהּ עַד כִּסֵּא כְבוֹדֶךָ וּסְתֹם פִּי הַמְקַטְרְגִים עָלֶיהָ וְיִכָּנְסוּ לְפָנֶיךָ כָּל הַמְלִיצִים בַּעֲדָהּ טוֹב כְּמִדָּתְךָ לְהֵטִיב לַהֲגוּן וּלְבִלְתִּי הָגוּן וְיִכָּמְרוּ רַחֲמֶיךָ עָלֶיהָ כִּי אַתָּה עוֹנֶה בְּעֵת צָרָה, מֶלֶךְ רַחֲמָן וּמְרַחֵם עַל כֻּלָּם, פּוֹדֶה וּמַצִּיל, שׁוֹמֵעַ וְעוֹנֶה.

**To be recited by the husband
when his wife is in active labor.
This prayer is preceded by
La-M'natzai'ach MizMor Le Dovid (Psalm 20)
which is to be said twelve times.**

(*Adapted from the Sefer Avodas Ha-Kodesh.*)

La-M'natzai'ach Mizmor Le Dovid
Psalm 20

For the Conductor, a psalm of David, God will answer you in the day of trouble: may the name of God of Jacob defend you. He will send forth your help from the sanctuary, and will strengthen you from Zion. May He remember all your offerings, and accept with favor your burnt offering. May He grant you your heart's desire, and fulfill all your counsel. May we rejoice in Your salvation, and in the name of our God set up our banner. May God fulfill all that you ask. Now I know that God saves His anointed; that He answers him from His holy heaven with the omnipotent acts of salvation of His right hand. Some trust in chariots and some in horses, but as for us, we remember the name of the Lord our God. They are bowed down and fallen, but we have always risen again and have constantly kept ourselves upright. May God grant salvation. The King will answer us on the day on which we call upon Him.

תפלה

כשהאשה יושבת על המשבר

(על פי ספר עבודת הקודש—סנסן ליאיר)

כשיושבת על המשבר יאמר שנים עשר פעמים מזמור יענך (תהלים כ')

ולא ישנה המזמור ללשון נקבה אלא יאמרנו ככתוב

למנצח מזמור לדוד

(תהלים כ')

לַמְנַצֵּחַ מִזְמוֹר לְדָוִד: יַעַנְךָ יי בְּיוֹם צָרָה, יְשַׂגֶּבְךָ שֵׁם אֱלֹהֵי יַעֲקֹב: יִשְׁלַח עֶזְרְךָ מִקֹּדֶשׁ, וּמִצִּיּוֹן יִסְעָדֶךָּ: יִזְכֹּר כָּל־מִנְחֹתֶיךָ, וְעוֹלָתְךָ יְדַשְּׁנֶה סֶלָה: יִתֶּן־לְךָ כִלְבָבֶךָ, וְכָל־עֲצָתְךָ יְמַלֵּא: נְרַנְּנָה בִּישׁוּעָתֶךָ, וּבְשֵׁם אֱלֹהֵינוּ נִדְגֹּל, יְמַלֵּא יי כָּל־מִשְׁאֲלוֹתֶיךָ: עַתָּה יָדַעְתִּי כִּי הוֹשִׁיעַ יי מְשִׁיחוֹ יַעֲנֵהוּ מִשְּׁמֵי קָדְשׁוֹ, בִּגְבֻרוֹת יֵשַׁע יְמִינוֹ: אֵלֶּה בָרֶכֶב וְאֵלֶּה בַסּוּסִים וַאֲנַחְנוּ בְּשֵׁם יי אֱלֹהֵינוּ נַזְכִּיר: הֵמָּה כָּרְעוּ וְנָפָלוּ, וַאֲנַחְנוּ קַמְנוּ וַנִּתְעוֹדָד: יי הוֹשִׁיעָה הַמֶּלֶךְ יַעֲנֵנוּ בְיוֹם קָרְאֵנוּ:

Prayer from *Sefer Avodas Ha-Kodesh*

May it be Your will O God, our God and God of our fathers. God of Abraham, God of Isaac, and God of Jacob, the great, mighty and awesome God. **EHEYE ASHER EHEYE** (I will ever be that which I now am.) Almighty, God of Hosts, may You act for the sake of Your great mercy, and for the sake of the holiness of this psalm, and for Your names that are written and included herein (within this psalm). May You have mercy on (the woman's name and mother's name) who is ready to deliver, crying out in her pains. O God, full of compassion, take her out of the darkness to the light. In the merit of our holy matriarchs, Sarah, Rebecca, Rachel and Leah, have mercy upon her and remember her for good. Bring blessing upon her, for her eyes depend on You, as a maidservant's eyes depend upon her mistress. Nullify any harsh or evil decrees that are upon her, with the name of *קרע שטן*, and save her from all pain. May the child be delivered to a good life, and for peace, at an appropriate and blessed time for us and for the child. Afterward, may the placenta deliver easily. Just as You have heeded the one who (originally) prayed this psalm before You, so may You heed our prayers. Act for the sake of Your name; act for the sake of Your right hand; act for the sake of Your Torah; act for the sake of Your holiness. May the One who answered his (*Dovid Hamelech*'s) mother answer me. May the words of my mouth and the meditation of my heart be pleasing before You, O God, my Rock and my Redeemer.

* The words themselves are not to be read, rather one should pronounce only the Hebrew letters individually:

koof, raish, ayin — sin, tes, nun.

תפילה מספר עבודת הקודש

יְהִי רָצוֹן מִלְּפָנֶיךָ יי אֱלֹהֵינוּ וֵאלֹהֵי אֲבוֹתֵינוּ אֱלֹהֵי אַבְרָהָם אֱלֹהֵי יִצְחָק וֵאלֹהֵי יַעֲקֹב הָאֵל הַגָּדוֹל הַגִּבּוֹר וְהַנּוֹרָא אֶהְיֶה אֲשֶׁר אֶהְיֶה שַׁדַּי צְבָאוֹת שֶׁתַּעֲשֶׂה לְמַעַן רַחֲמֶיךָ הָרַבִּים וּלְמַעַן קְדֻשַּׁת הַמִּזְמוֹר הַזֶּה וּשְׁמוֹתֶיךָ הַכְּתוּבִים בּוֹ וְהַמְצֹרָפִים בּוֹ וּתְרַחֵם עַל (פְּלוֹנִית בַּת פְּלוֹנִית) הַיּוֹשֶׁבֶת עַל הַמַּשְׁבֵּר צוֹעֶקֶת בַּחֲבָלֶיהָ. אֵל מָלֵא רַחֲמִים תּוֹצִיאָהּ מֵאֲפֵלָה לְאוֹרָה וּבִזְכוּת אִמּוֹתֵינוּ הַקְּדוֹשׁוֹת, שָׂרָה רִבְקָה רָחֵל וְלֵאָה, תְּרַחֵם עָלֶיהָ וְתִזְכְּרֶנָּה לְטוֹבָה וְתִפְקְדֶנָּה לִבְרָכָה כִּי עֵינֶיהָ לְךָ תְלוּיוֹת כְּעֵינֵי שִׁפְחָה אֶל יַד גְּבִרְתָּהּ וּתְבַטֵּל מֵעָלֶיהָ כָּל-גְּזֵרוֹת קָשׁוֹת וְרָעוֹת בְּשֵׁם *קְרַע שָׂטָן* וְתַצִּילֶהָ מִכָּל-צַעַר וְיֵצֵא הַוָּלָד לְחַיִּים טוֹבִים וּלְשָׁלוֹם וּבְשָׁעָה טוֹבָה וּמְבֹרֶכֶת לָנוּ וְלַוָּלָד וְאַחַר-כָּךְ תֵּצֵא הַשִּׁלְיָא בְּנָקֵל וּכְשֵׁם שֶׁשָּׁמַעְתָּ מִי שֶׁהִתְפַּלֵּל לְפָנֶיךָ הַמִּזְמוֹר הַזֶּה כֵּן תִּשְׁמַע תְּפִלָּתֵנוּ עֲשֵׂה לְמַעַן שְׁמֶךָ עֲשֵׂה לְמַעַן יְמִינֶךָ עֲשֵׂה לְמַעַן תּוֹרָתֶךָ עֲשֵׂה לְמַעַן קְדֻשָּׁתֶךָ. מַאן דְּעָנֵי לְאִמָּךְ הוּא יַעֲנֶה יָתָךְ. יִהְיוּ לְרָצוֹן אִמְרֵי פִי וְהֶגְיוֹן לִבִּי לְפָנֶיךָ יי צוּרִי וְגוֹאֲלִי.

*לא לקרא את המלים רק לבטא את האותיות: קוף, ריש, עין — שין, טית, נון

To be recited by the husband
at some time during his wife's pregnancy.

(Taken from Sefer Bais Tefillah.)

Master of the Universe! I thank You for your graciousness towards me and for granting my wife pregnancy. May the Name of God be blessed and uplifted above all blessing and praise. Therefore, may it be Your will, our God, and God of our fathers, that You have mercy on all the pregnant women in Your nation, Israel. May You ease the suffering of their pregnancy, and spare them from miscarrying their fetuses. May You spare those that are ready to deliver, all evil. In Your abundant compassion, let them give birth to [children that will have] a good life. Among them may Your compassion come forth on behalf of my wife, Your maidservant (the woman's name and mother's name). May You ease the suffering of her pregnancy, and when the term of her pregnancy is fulfilled, may she give birth easily, and let the child be born into the world at an appropriate time with good fortune for us and for the child. Let no sickness or blemish affect the mother or the child. May the fetus be complete in all his limbs and his senses. May goodness be decreed upon him, and let him have good fortune. I will rejoice in my offspring, and my wife will be glad with her children in this world and in the world to come, so that we may neither be ashamed nor embarrassed, nor stumble for ever and ever. In Your great, mighty and awesome holy name we trust, God full of mercy. Fill Yourself with mercy for us, and seal the mouth of the accuser so that he should not accuse my wife when the time comes for her to give birth. All those that rise up against us for evil, let terror and dread fall upon them.

תפלה
למי שאשתו מעוברת

(לקח מספר בית תפילה)

רִבּוֹנוֹ שֶׁל עוֹלָם מוֹדֶה אֲנִי לְפָנֶיךָ עַל שֶׁחוֹנַנְתָּנִי וְנָתַתָּ לַאֲמָתְךָ אִשְׁתִּי הֵרָיוֹן יְהִי שֵׁם יי מְבֹרָךְ וּמְרוֹמָם עַל כָּל בְּרָכָה וּתְהִלָּה. וּבְכֵן יְהִי רָצוֹן מִלְּפָנֶיךָ יי אֱלֹהֵינוּ וֵאלֹהֵי אֲבוֹתֵינוּ שֶׁתְּרַחֵם עַל־כָּל־עֻבָּרוֹת עַמְּךָ יִשְׂרָאֵל וְתָקֵל מֵעֲלֵיהֶן צַעַר עִבּוּרָן וְתַצִּילֵן שֶׁלֹּא תַּפֵּלְנָה וְלָדוֹתֵיהֶן. וְהַיּוֹשְׁבוֹת עַל הַמַּשְׁבֵּר בְּרַחֲמֶיךָ הָרַבִּים תַּצִּילֵן מִכָּל־רַע וְתֵלַדְנָה לְחַיִּים טוֹבִים וּבִכְלָלָן יֶהֱמוּ נָא רַחֲמֶיךָ עַל אֲמָתְךָ אִשְׁתִּי (פְּלוֹנִית בַּת פְּלוֹנִית) וְתָקֵל מֵעָלֶיהָ צַעַר עִבּוּרָהּ, וּבִמְלֹאת יָמֶיהָ לָלֶדֶת תֵּלֵד בְּנָקֵל וְיֵצֵא הַוָּלָד לַאֲוִיר הָעוֹלָם בְּשָׁעָה טוֹבָה וּבְמַזָּל טוֹב לָנוּ וְלַוָּלָד וְלֹא יֶאֱרַע שׁוּם חֳלִי וְשׁוּם מוּם לֹא לַיּוֹלֶדֶת וְלֹא לַוָּלָד. וְיִהְיֶה הַוָּלָד שָׁלֵם בְּכָל־אֵבָרָיו וּבְכָל־חוּשָׁיו וְתִגְזוֹר עָלָיו גְּזֵרוֹת טוֹבוֹת וְיִהְיֶה בְּרִיָּא מַזָּלֵיהּ. וְאֶשְׂמַח אֲנִי בְּיוֹצְאֵי חֲלָצַי וְתָגֵל אִשְׁתִּי בִּפְרִי בִטְנָהּ בָּעוֹלָם הַזֶּה וּבְעוֹלָם הַבָּא. וְלֹא נֵבוֹשׁ וְלֹא נִכָּלֵם וְלֹא נִכָּשֵׁל לְעוֹלָם וָעֶד בְּשֵׁם קָדְשְׁךָ הַגָּדוֹל הַגִּבּוֹר וְהַנּוֹרָא בָּטַחְנוּ. אֵל מָלֵא רַחֲמִים הִתְמַלֵּא בְּרַחֲמִים עָלֵינוּ חֲתֹם פֶּה שָׂטָן וְאַל יַשְׂטִין עַל אִשְׁתִּי בְּעֵת לְדָתָהּ. וְכָל־הַקָּמִים עָלֵינוּ לְרָעָה תַּפֵּל עֲלֵיהֶם אֵימָתָה

When Your arm shows its greatness, they grow still as a stone. May Your compassion hasten to our aid, for we are brought very low. Master of compassion, deal with us with the attribute of kindness and the attribute of mercy, and may we be entered beyond the requirement of the law. Do not enter into judgment with us, and do not judge us according to our misdeeds. Deal with us in clemency and loving-kindness for the sake of Your great name, and grant us long life to do Your service. May my wife and I be found worthy so that we grow old together in Your service in the holy land. We will rejoice with our offspring when we see them doing Your will, as is Your wish. We will complete the perfection of *NEFESH, RUACH, NESHAMA* (Life, Spirit, Soul) in this transmigration. May we merit to live and inherit goodness and blessing for the world to come, so that the soul may sing praise to You, and not be silent. O Lord, my God, forever will I give thanks to You. Do it for the sake of Your abundant mercies and for the sake of our holy fathers, Abraham, Isaac, and Israel, Your servants, for the sake of Moses, Aaron, Joseph and David, and for the sake of all the righteous, may their merit shield us. Do it for Your sake, not for ours. May the words of my mouth and the meditation of my heart be pleasing before You, O God, my Rock and my Redeemer.

נָפַחַד בְּגֹדֶל זְרוֹעֲךָ יִדְּמוּ כָּאָבֶן. מַהֵר יְקַדְּמוּנוּ רַחֲמֶיךָ כִּי דַלּוֹנוּ מְאֹד.
בַּעַל הָרַחֲמִים הִתְנַהֵג עִמָּנוּ בְּמִדַּת הַחֶסֶד וּבְמִדַּת הָרַחֲמִים וְתִכָּנֵס
לָנוּ לִפְנַי וְלִפְנִים מִשּׁוּרַת הַדִּין וְאַל תָּבֹא בְמִשְׁפָּט עִמָּנוּ וְאַל תְּדִינֵנוּ
כְּמַעֲלָלֵנוּ. עֲשֵׂה עִמָּנוּ צְדָקָה וָחֶסֶד לְמַעַן שִׁמְךָ הַגָּדוֹל. וְתֵן לָנוּ חַיִּים
אֲרוּכִים לַעֲבוֹדָתֶךָ, וּתְזַכֵּנוּ לִי וּלְאִשְׁתִּי שֶׁנַּזְקִין יַחַד בָּאָרֶץ הַקְּדוֹשָׁה
בַּעֲבוֹדָתֶךָ. וְנִשְׂמַח בְּיוֹצְאֵי חֲלָצֵינוּ בִּרְאוֹתֵנוּ אוֹתָם עוֹשִׂים רְצוֹנְךָ
כִּרְצוֹנֶךָ וְנַשְׁלִים תִּקּוּן נֶפֶשׁ רוּחַ נְשָׁמָה בְּגִלְגּוּל זֶה. וְנִזְכֶּה וְנִחְיֶה
וְנִירַשׁ טוֹבָה וּבְרָכָה לְחַיֵּי הָעוֹלָם הַבָּא לְמַעַן יְזַמֶּרְךָ כָבוֹד וְלֹא יִדֹּם
יי אֱלֹהַי לְעוֹלָם אוֹדֶךָ. עֲשֵׂה לְמַעַן רַחֲמֶיךָ הָרַבִּים וּלְמַעַן אֲבוֹתֵינוּ
הַקְּדוֹשִׁים אַבְרָהָם יִצְחָק וְיִשְׂרָאֵל עֲבָדֶיךָ וּלְמַעַן מֹשֶׁה וְאַהֲרֹן יוֹסֵף
דָּוִד וּלְמַעַן כָּל־הַצַּדִּיקִים זְכוּתָם יָגֵן עָלֵינוּ עֲשֵׂה לְמַעַנְךָ לֹא
לְמַעֲנֵנוּ. יִהְיוּ לְרָצוֹן אִמְרֵי פִי וְהֶגְיוֹן לִבִּי לְפָנֶיךָ ה׳ צוּרִי וְגוֹאֲלִי.

To be said by the woman herself
sometime during pregnancy.

(*Taken from the Sefer **Shaarei Dimah**.*)

May it be Your will, O God, and God of my fathers, that
You ease the suffering of my pregnancy, and continue to give
me strength and power during the term of my pregnancy, that
my strength and the strength of the fetus should not weaken in
any manner at all. Save me from the fate of Chava, and from
the curse of "I will greatly multiply the pains of your child-
bearing. In sorrow you will bear children." (Genesis 2:16) At
the time that I am ready to give birth, when the term of my
pregnancy is complete, may my labor pains not be unduly
oppressive, and may the child be born into the world without
delay, easily, and without any damage to me or to the child.
The child should be born at an appropriate time, with good
fortune, for a good life, for peace and good health, for favor
and kindness, for wealth and honor. May the statement that is
written "There should neither be a woman that miscarries nor a
barren woman in your land; the number of your days I will fill
[with good]" (Exodus 23:26) be fulfilled in me. My husband
and I will rise to do Your service and to learn Your holy
Torah, for a good life, peace and wealth, happiness, honor
and serenity. May it not occur that I or the unborn child be
damaged bodily, not in the limbs, and not the sinews, and not
the blood vessels, and not the skin or flesh, or in the rest of the
composition of man. Not within the hollow of the body, and not
on the outside of the body. Strengthen me, my spirit and my
bones, as it states "It should be health to your navel and
marrow to your bones." (Proverbs 3:8) Because to You, God, I
hoped; You will answer, God, my God. And I will rejoice in

תפלה
לאשה מעוברת

(לקח מספר שערי דמעה)

יְהִי רָצוֹן מִלְפָנֶיךָ, יְיָ אֱלֹהַי וֵאלֹהֵי אֲבוֹתַי, שֶׁתָּקֵל מֵעָלַי אֶת־צַעַר
עִבּוּרִי, וְתוֹסִיף וְתִתֵּן לִי כֹּחַ וָאוֹן בְּכָל יְמֵי הָעִבּוּר, שֶׁלֹּא יִתַּשׁ כֹּחִי
וְלֹא כֹחַ הָעֻבָּר בְּשׁוּם דָּבָר בָּעוֹלָם וְתַצִּיל אוֹתִי מִפְּתִיקָה שֶׁל־חַנָּה,
וּמִקְלָלַת הָרְבָּה אַרְבֶּה עִצְּבוֹנֵךְ וְהֵרֹנֵךְ בְּעֶצֶב תֵּלְדִי בָנִים. וִיהִי בְעֵת
לֵדָתִי כִּי יִמְלְאוּ יָמַי לָלֶדֶת, לֹא יֵהָפְכוּ עָלַי צִירָי. וְיֵצֵא הַנּוֹלָד לַאֲוִיר
הָעוֹלָם בְּרֶגַע קָטָן בְּקַלּוּת בְּלִי שׁוּם הֶזֵּק לֹא לִי וְלֹא לַנּוֹלָד. וְיִהְיֶה
נוֹלָד בְּשָׁעָה טוֹבָה וּבְמַזָּל טוֹב, לְחַיִּים טוֹבִים וּלְשָׁלוֹם וְלִבְרִיאוּת,
לְחֵן וּלְחֶסֶד, לְעֹשֶׁר וְכָבוֹד. וִיקֻיַּם בִּי מִקְרָא שֶׁכָּתוּב, לֹא תִהְיֶה
מְשַׁכֵּלָה וַעֲקָרָה בְּאַרְצֶךָ אֶת־מִסְפַּר יָמֶיךָ אֲמַלֵּא. וַאֲנִי וּבַעֲלִי נִגְדְּלֵהוּ
לַעֲבוֹדָתְךָ וּלְתוֹרָתְךָ הַקְּדוֹשָׁה, וּלְחַיִּים טוֹבִים וּלְשָׁלוֹם וְעֹשֶׁר וְאֹשֶׁר
וְכָבוֹד וּמְנוּחָה. וְלֹא נִהְיֶה לֹא אֲנִי וְלֹא הָעֻבָּר נִזּוֹקִים, לֹא בַגּוּף וְלֹא
בָאֵבָרִים וְלֹא בָעוֹרְקִים וְלֹא בַגִּידִים וְלֹא בָעוֹר וּבָשָׂר וּשְׁאָר כָּל־
בִּנְיַן בְּנֵי־אָדָם, לֹא בְתוֹךְ חֲלַל הַגּוּף וְלֹא חוּץ לַחֲלַל הַגּוּף. וּתְחַזֵּק
אֶת־כֹּחִי וְרוּחִי וְעַצְמוֹתַי, כְּמוֹ שֶׁנֶּאֱמַר, רִפְאוּת תְּהִי לְשָׁרֶּךָ וְשִׁקּוּי
לְעַצְמוֹתֶיךָ. כִּי לְךָ יְיָ הוֹחָלְתִּי, אַתָּה תַעֲנֶה יְיָ אֱלֹהָי. וַאֲנִי בְּיְ

God, I will be happy in the God of my salvation. God, desire to save me; God, hasten to help me. Hasten to help me, God of my salvation. For Your salvation do I hope, O God; O God, hear my voice. I call to You, and be gracious unto me and answer me. Act for the sake of our holy fathers and for the sake of their merits, and their righteousness, and for the sake of their Torah, and for the good deeds of those who are lying in the dust that are buried here and throughout the world. Remember their love [for You] and give life to their descendants, and save them from death and from miscarrying, from all sickness and sufferings. Bless me as You promised us in Your holy Torah that was given [to us] through the hand of Moses, Your servant, from the mouth of Your Glory. As it states, "And He will love you and bless you and multiply you, and He will bless the fruit of your body and the fruit of your soul, your grain, your wine, your oil, the offspring of your cattle, and the abundance of your sheep, upon the land which He swore to your fathers to give to you. You shall be blessed more than all the people; there shall not be found a barren male or a barren female among you or among your cattle." (Deuteronomy 7:13—14) So should You bless me and answer me, and favor me, and prolong my days with sweetness as it states, "I will satisfy him with length of days and let him behold my salvation." (Psalms 91:16)

אֶעֱלוֹזָה, אָגִילָה בֵּאלֹהֵי יִשְׁעִי. רְצֵה יי לְהַצִּילֵנִי, יי לְעֶזְרָתִי חוּשָׁה. חוּשָׁה לְעֶזְרָתִי יי תְּשׁוּעָתִי. לִישׁוּעָתְךָ קִוִּיתִי יי. שְׁמַע יי קוֹלִי אֶקְרָא וְחָנֵּנִי וַעֲנֵנִי. עֲשֵׂה לְמַעַן אֲבוֹתֵינוּ הַקְּדוֹשִׁים וּלְמַעַן זְכוּתָם וְצִדְקָתָם וּלְמַעַן תּוֹרָתָם וּמַעֲשֵׂיהֶם הַטּוֹבִים שֶׁל שׁוֹכְנֵי עָפָר הַטְּמוּנִים פֹּה וּבְכָל־הָעוֹלָם, תִּזְכֹּר אַהֲבָתָם וּתְחַיֶּה זַרְעָם וְתַצִּיל אוֹתָם מִמֶּוֶת וּמִמִּשְׁכֶּלֶת וּמִכָּל־חֳלִי וּמַדְוֶה. וּתְבָרְכֵנִי כַּאֲשֶׁר הִבְטַחְתָּנוּ בְּתוֹרָתְךָ הַקְּדוֹשָׁה עַל יְדֵי מֹשֶׁה עַבְדְּךָ מִפִּי כְבוֹדֶךָ כָּאָמוּר, וַאֲהֵבְךָ וּבֵרַכְךָ וְהִרְבֶּךָ וּבֵרַךְ פְּרִי בִטְנְךָ וּפְרִי אַדְמָתֶךָ דְּגָנְךָ וְתִירֹשְׁךָ וְיִצְהָרֶךָ שְׁגַר־אֲלָפֶיךָ וְעַשְׁתְּרֹת צֹאנֶךָ עַל הָאֲדָמָה אֲשֶׁר־נִשְׁבַּע לַאֲבֹתֶיךָ לָתֶת לָךְ. בָּרוּךְ תִּהְיֶה מִכָּל־הָעַמִּים לֹא־יִהְיֶה בְךָ עָקָר וַעֲקָרָה וּבִבְהֶמְתֶּךָ. כֵּן תְּבָרְכֵנִי וְתַעֲנֵנִי וּתְחַנְּנִי וְתַאֲרִיךְ יָמַי בַּנְּעִימִים, כָּאָמוּר, אֹרֶךְ יָמִים אַשְׂבִּיעֵהוּ וְאַרְאֵהוּ בִּישׁוּעָתִי אָמֵן:

A prayer for a woman in labor
that others should recite on her behalf

(Taken from the Sefer **Techina Kol Bo HaChodosh***)*

Master of the universe! We come before You with broken
hearts and eyes full of tears on behalf of (the woman's name and
mother's name), who must now give birth to her child. We
beseech You, O merciful God, to have compassion on her, that
she give birth quickly, easily and painlessly. Since the key of
childbirth is in Your hands, and You have infinite mercy over
all Your creatures, have mercy on this woman, and look at the
tears we have shed on her behalf. The gates of tears are not
locked, and You hearkened to the prayer of our father,
Abraham, when he prayed for the wife and maidservants of
Abimelech that they should give birth and, indeed, they gave
birth easily, although they were idol worshippers. Now we come
before You on behalf of this Jewish woman, who worships You,
O merciful and gracious God, please open her womb quickly

אֵיין תְּחִנָה פַאר אַ יוֹלֶדֶת אַנְדֶערֶע זָאלִין פַאר אִיר בֶּעטִין

(גענומען פון דעם ספר תחינה כל בו החדש)

רִבּוֹנוֹ שֶׁל עוֹלָם מִיר זֶענִין אִיצְט גֶעקוּמֶען פַאר דִיר מִיט
צוּבְּרָאכֶענֶע הֶערצֶער אוּן מִיט פִיל טְרֶערִין פַארגִיסִין, פוּן װֶעגִין
דִי אִשָּׁה (פְּלוֹנִית בַּת פְּלוֹנִית) וואָס זִי דַארְף אִיצְט גִיבָּארִין אִיר
קִינָד, דוּ לִיבֶּער רַחֲמָנוּתדִיגֶער גָאט זָאלְסְט אוֹיף אִיר רַחֲמָנוּת
הָאבִּין זִי זָאל גִישְׁוִוינְט אוּן גְרִינְג גִיבָּארִין אָן צַער אוּן אָן
יִסוּרִים, דֶען דֶער שְׁלִיסֶל פוּן אַ גֶעוִוינֶערִין אִיז דָאךְ נָאר אִין דַיין
הַאנְט, אוּן דַיינֶע רַחֲמָנוּת זֶענִין דָאךְ גְרוֹיס אוֹיף יֶעדֶער
בַּאשֶׁעפֶענִיש, הָאב רַחֲמָנוּת אוֹיף דִי אִשָּׁה אוּן זָאלְסְט זֶעהָן
אוּנזֶערֶע טְרֶערִין וואָס מִיר וִוינִין אוּן פַארגִיסִין פוּן אִירֶעטְװֶעגִין,
אוּן אַזוֹי וִוי דִי טוֹיעֶרִין פוּן טְרֶערִין זֶענִין נִיט פַארשְׁלָאסִין, אוּן
אַזוֹי וִוי דוּ הָאסְט אָנְגֶענוּמֶין דִי תְּפִלָה פוּן אַבְרָהָם אָבִינוּ װֶען עֶר
הָאט גִיבֶּעטִין פַאר דָאס װַייב אוּן דִי דִינְסְטִין פוּן אֲבִימֶלֶךְ זֵיי זָאלִין
גִיבָּארִין זֵייעֶרֶע קִינָדֶער, אוּן זֵיי הָאבִּין גְרִינְג גִיבָּארִין וואָס זֵיי
זֶענִין גִיװֶוען גֶעצִין דִינֶער, אוּן מִיר זֶענִין אִיצְט גֶעקוּמִין פַאר דִיר
רַחוּם וְחַנוּן בֶּעטִין דוּ זָאלְסְט רַחֲמָנוּת הָאבְּן אוֹיף דִי אִידִישֶׁע
פְרוֹי וואָס זִי דִינְט צוּ דִיר רַחוּם וְחַנוּן, דוּ זָאלְסְט עֶפֶּענִין אִיר

and painlessly. Just as You saved all righteous women from the curse imposed on *Chavah,* so shall You save this woman, and grant her long life. Make her a mother of a living child, which she is now ready to deliver. May she merit to raise him to Torah, marriage and good deeds. If, God forbid, she has committed sins, accept her present repentance. You are close to anyone who calls upon You sincerely and wholeheartedly, and when a person is in grave danger, God forbid, You help him. In the merit of her saintly parents and in the merit of our commandments and good deeds as well as her commandments and good deeds, accept our prayers that we pray on her behalf and the tears that we shed for her, and close the mouths of all her accusers and summon good angels to defend her, so that in her house, joyful voices will soon be heard on the occasion of the birth of this child. Amen.

מוטער לײַב גישװוינט און גרינג אָן צער און אָן יסורים, און אזוי
װי דו האָסט גערעטעט אַלע פרומע װײַבער פון חנה'ס קללה אזוי
זאָלסטו די אשה אויך רעטין, און זי זאָל לאָנג לעבין און זיין אַ
מוטער צו דאָס לעבעדיגע קינד נאָר װאָס זי װעט איצט געבאָרין זי
זאָל אים אויפהאָדעװען צו תּורה חופּה און מעשׂים טובים, און
װען חס ושלום זי האָט עפּעס געזינדיגט, זאָלסטו אָן נעמין איר
איצטיגע תּשובה, דו ביזט נאָנט צו יעדער מענטש װאָס
רופט צו דיר מיט אמת און מיט זיין גאַנצע האַרץ, און װען
אַמענטש איז חס ושלום אין די גרעסטע צרה ביזטו דאָך זיין
העלפער און אין דעם זכות פון איך הײליגע עלטערין. און אין
דעם זכות פון אונזערע מצות און מעשׂים טובים און אין דעם
זכות פון איך מצות און מעשׂים טובים זאָלסטו אָן נעמין
אונזערע טרערין און װיינין און בעטין און װאָס מיר בעטין פאר
איךעטװעגין, און זאָלסט פאַרמאַכין די מײַלער פון אַלע
מקטריגים װאָס זענין מקטרג אויף איר, און זאָלסט הײסין קומין
פאר דיר אַלע גוטע מליצים פון איךעטװעגין, און עס זאָל באַלד
גיהערט װערין אין שטוב שׂמחה וששון מיט דעם נײַעם
גיבאָרינעם קינד, אמן:

To be recited by a woman
when she goes into labor

*(Taken from the Sefer **Techina Kol Bo HaChodosh**)*

Master of the Universe! Have pity on me and accept my prayer, which I tearfully and brokenheartedly pray before You. Pay heed to my sighs and my weeping and forgive me the sins that I have committed against You. O merciful Father, have pity on me as a father has pity on his child. Give me strength to give birth to my child quickly and without injury either to me or to my child. Just as You have helped all good and pious women, and as You helped my mother, help me too. No one can help me but You. I beseech You from the bottom of my heart that You send me Your help, so that I should give birth to this child quickly and painlessly. Just as You created the world with the sole purpose of bestowing kindness, show me Your kindness, that I should give birth to a living child and that I should be a

אַיין תְּחִנָה פַאר אַ יוֹלֶדֶת זי זָאל אַלֵיין זָאגֶין בְּעֵת זי פִילט אַז זי גֵייט צו קינד

(גענומען פון דעם ספר תחינה כל בו החדש)

רִבּוֹנוֹ שֶׁל עוֹלָם, הֶער פוּן דִי גַאנְצֶע וֶועלְט הָאב רַחֲמָנוּת
אויף מִיר אוּן פַארְנֶעם מַיין גֶעבֶּעט ווָאס אִיךְ טוּה בֶּעטְין פַאר
דִיר מִיט מַיינֶע טְרֶערֶין אוּן מִיט מַיין צוּבְּרָאכִין הַארְץ, אוּן
פַארְנֶעם מַיין זיפְצִין אוּן מַיין וֵויינִין. אוּן זַיי מִיר מוֹחֵל ווָאס אִיךְ
הָאב גֶעגִין דִיר גֶעזִינְדִיגְט דֶערבַּארֶעמְדִיגֶער פָאטֶער הָאב
רַחֲמָנוּת אויף מִיר ווי אַ פָאטֶער הָאט רַחֲמָנוּת אויף זַיין קִינְד, אוּן
גִיב מִיר כֹּח אוּן קְרָאפְט אִיךְ זָאל גֶעשְׁווִינְט גֶעבָּארִין דָאס קִינְד,
אוּן עֶס זָאל קֵיין שָׁאדִין נִיט זַיין אִין מִיר אוּן נִיט דֶעם קִינְד, אוּן
אַזוֹי ווי דוּ הָאסְט גֶיהָאלְפִין צוּ אַלֶע גוּטֶע אוּן פְרוּמֶע ווַיבֶּער אוּן
אַזוֹי ווי דוּ הָאסְט גֶיהָאלְפִין מַיין מוּטֶער הֶעלְף מִיר אויךְ, דֶען
עֶס אִיז קֵיין אַנְדֶער נִיט דָא ווָאס זָאל מִיר קֶעגנִין הֶעלְפִין נָאר דוּ
אַלֵיין, אִיךְ בֶּעט צוּ דִיר פוּן טִיפְסְטִין הַארְצִין דוּ זָאלְסְט שִׁיקִין צוּ
מִיר דַיין גְרוֹיסֶע הִילְף, אִיךְ זָאל גֶעבָּארִין דָאס קִינְד גֶעשְׁווִינְט אָן
שְׁמֶערְצִין, אוּן אַזוֹי ווי דוּ הָאסְט בַּאשַׁאפִין דִי גַאנְצֶע ווֶעלְט נָאר
צוּ טָאהְן זֵיי חֶסֶד, ווַייז מִיר אויךְ דַיינֶע חֲסָדִים, אִיךְ זָאל גֶעבָּארִין
אַ לֶעבֶּעדִיג קִינְד אוּן אִיךְ זָאל זַיין אַ מוּטֶער צוּ דֶעם קִינְד, עֶס אִיז

mother to this child. True, You created women that they should bring children into the world, and You punished the first woman that she should bear children in pain. Nevertheless, you retained the key of childbirth so that not all women should be punished, but those upon whom You have compassion are redeemed from that punishment. Therefore, I beseech You, O merciful Father, since I am now in Your hands, help me to live and to bear this child to live, and with my tears, wash away my sins. May defending angels and the merit of the Patriarchs come before you and beg for me that my child and I shall have life and peace.

אֱמֶת דוּ הָאסְט בַּשַׁאפִין דִי וַויבֶּער זֵיי זָאלִין גִיבָּארִין אוּן
בְּרֵיינְגִין מֶענְשִׁין אוֹיף דֶער וֶועלְט, אוּן דָאס עֶרְשְׁטֶע וַויבּ חַוָה
הָאסְטוּ גֶעשְׁטְרָאפְט זִי זָאל גִיבָּארִין אִירֶע קִינְדֶער מִיט שְׁמֶערְצִין.
נָאר דֶערִיבֶּער הָאסְט דוּ גֶענוּמִין דֶעם שְׁלִיסֶעל פוּן דִי גֶעוַוינֶערְנְם
אִין דַיין הַאנְט, דָאס נִיט אַלֶע וַוייבֶּער זָאלִין גִישְׁטְרָאפְט וֶוערִין
מִיט דִי שְׁטְרָאף. נָאר אוֹיף וֶועמִין דַיינֶע רַחְמָנוּת וֶועט זַיין זִי
וֶועט אוֹיסְגֶעלֵייזְט וֶוערִין פוּן דִי שְׁטְרָאף, דֶערִיבֶּער בֶּעט אִיךְ דִיךְ
רַחֲמָנוּתדִיגֶער פָאטֶער אַזוֹי וִוי אִיךְ בִּין אִיצְט אִין דַיין הַאנְט
זָאלְסְטוּ מִיר הֶעלְפִין צוּם לֵעבִּין אוּן אִיךְ זָאל דָאס קִינְד גִיבָּארִין
צוּם לֵעבִּין, אוּן מִיט מַיינֶע טְרֶערִין זָאלְסְטוּ אָפְּוַואשִׁין אוּן
אָפְּמֶעקְין מַיינֶע זִינְד, אוּן עֶס זָאל קוּמִין פַאר דִיר מְלִיצִים טוֹבִים
אוּן זְכוּת אָבוֹת אוּן בְּעטִין פוּן מַיינֶעטְוֶועגִין אִיךְ מִיט דָאס קִינְד
זָאלִין מִיר זַיין לְחַיִים וּלְשָׁלוֹם:

**To be recited by a woman
who has recovered from childbirth
and has gone to *shule* for the first time**
(*Taken from the Sefer* **Techina Kol Bo HaChodosh**)

O merciful and forgiving God! You are the Master of mercy and forgiveness. I thank You, O God, for saving me from the bitter pangs of childbirth and for letting me live to recover from my ordeal. In days of yore, when the Temple existed, I would have had to come to the Temple to thank You by offering up sacrifices. Now, that the Temple is no longer in existence, the synagogue is like the Temple, our prayers are the sacrifices and our tears are the wine libations. Therefore, I beseech You, O Lord of the Universe, accept my speech and my prayers and my calling upon Your Holy Name from the bottom of my heart in lieu of sacrifices and meal offerings. Protect me further from all harm, give me strength to nourish my child and help my husband and me with long life, health and sustenance, so that we will be able to raise this child and all our children to the study of

אייַן תְּחִנָה פַאר אַ פְרוֹי וֶוען זי שְטייט אויף פון
קינדבֶּעט און גייט אין שוּהל דָאס עֶרְשְטֶע מָאל

(גענומֶען פון דעם ספר תחינה כל בו החדש)

אֲדוֹן הָרַחֲמִים וְהַסְלִיחוֹת. דו בִּיזְט דֶער הֶער פון די רַחֲמָנוּת
און פון די זִינְד פַארְגֶעבּוּנְג, אִיך דַאנְק דיר גָאט פַאר די רֶעטוּנְג
וֶוואס דו הָאסְט מִיך גֶירֶעטֶעט פון די בִּיטֶערֶע שְמֶערְצִין און
הָאסְט מִיך גֶעלָאזְט לֶעבּין און דו הָאסְט מִיר גִיגֶעבּין נייַע
קרֶעפְטִין אִיך זָאל קֶענִין אויפְשְטייַן פון דֶעם בֶּעט, פַארְצייַטִין
וֶוען דֶער בֵּית הַמִקְדָש אִיז גֶיוֶוען הָאבּ אִיך גִידַארְפְט קומִין אִין
בֵּית הַמִקְדָש דיר גֶעבּין מייַן דַאנְק, און בְּרֵיינְגִין קָרְבָּנוֹת הייַנְט אַז
דֶער בֵּית הַמִקְדָש אִיז נִיטָא, וֶוערְט גִירֶעכְונְט די שוּהל וֶוי אַבֵּית
הַמִקְדָש. און די תְּפִלוֹת זֶענִין די קָרְבָּנוֹת. און די טְרֶערִין זייַנִין די
וֶויַן פון די קָרְבָּנוֹת. דֶערִיבֶּער בֶּעט אִיך דִיךְ רִבּוֹנוֹ שֶל עוֹלָם נֶעם
אָן מייַנֶע רֵייד און מייַן גִיבֶּעט און מייַן אָן רופִין דייַן הֵיילִיגִין
נָאמִין פון טִיפִין הַארְצִין אַזוֹי וִוי קָרְבָּנוֹת און מְנָחוֹת. און בֶּעהִיט
מִיךְ וֶוייַטֶער פון אַלֶעם בֵּייז און גִיב מִיר כֹּח און קְרַאפְט אִיך זָאל
קֶענִין דֶערְנֶערְין דָאס קִינְד, און הֶעלְף אוּנְז מִיר און מייַן מַאן מִיט
לַאנְג לֶעבּין גֶעזוּנְד און פַּרְנָסָה מִיר זָאלִין קֶענִין אויפְהָאדֶעווֶען
דָאס קִינְד און אוּנְזֶערֶע אַלֶע קִינְדֶער צו תּוֹרָה לֶערְנִין און צו יִרְאַת

Torah, the fear of God, to the nuptial canopy and to the performance of good deeds, to wealth and honor. In our home, there should be only good luck, blessing and prosperity. We should never have sickness in our home. Only joy and happiness should be heard. Concerning that matter, I have come to the synagogue to thank You for the benefits You have bestowed on my husband and me until this day, and I beg You to continue bestowing kindness upon us. May it be Your will, O God, that we merit to see the rebuilding of the Holy Temple and that we bring real sacrifices with song and joy to the Holy One, blessed be He.*

* The woman should give as much charity as she can or her husband should give charity on her behalf.

שָׁמַיִם. צוּ חוּפָּה אוּן צוּ מַעֲשִׂים טוֹבִים. צוּ עוֹשֶׁר וְכָבוֹד. אִין
אוּנְזֶער שְׁטוּב זָאל נָאר זַיין מַזָל אוּן בְּרָכָה וְהַצְלָחָה. עֶם זָאל קֵיין
קְרַאנְקַייט זַיין אִין אוּנְזֶער שְׁטוּב, עֶס זָאל בַּיי אוּנְז גִיהֶערְט וֶוערִין
נָאר שָׂשׂוֹן וְשִׂמְחָה. אוּן וֶועגִין דֶעם בִּין אִיךְ גִיקוּמִין אִין שׁוּהְל דִיר
דַאנְקִין פַאר דִי טוֹבוֹת וָואס דוּ הָאסְט גִיטָאהְן מִיט מִיר אוּן מִיט
מַיין מַאן אוּן קִינְדֶער בִּיז הַיינְט, אוּן בֶּעט אוֹיף וַוייטֶער מִיט אוּנְז
צוּ טָאהְן חֲסָדִים. אוּן עֶס זָאל זַיין דֶער וִוילְין פַאר דִיר גָאט מִיר
זָאלְין זוֹכֶה זַיין צוּ זֶעהְן וִוי דֶער בֵּית הַמִּקְדָּשׁ וֶועט גִיבּוֹיט וֶוערִין
אוּן מִיר זָאלְין בְּרֵיינְגִין אֶמֶתְעַ קָרְבָּנוֹת מִיט גֶעזַאנְג אוּן לוֹיב צוּ
הקב״ה:*

*) דיא אשה זאל געבין צדקה וויא פיל זיא קען געבין, אדער דער מאן זאל געבין
צדקה פאר איר.

סגולות ועצות

* * * * * * *

SPIRITUAL REMEDIES
AND ADVICE

**The following *segulos*,
which are found in various holy books,
were intended for the purpose of
minimizing the pain a woman might have during childbirth.**

A woman must be specially careful in fulfilling the *mitzvos* of *niddah, challah* and candle lighting.

Based on *Tractate Shabbos Chapter 2 Mishnah 6*
* * * * *

If a woman is having difficulty during childbirth, one should not discuss her sins. She should repent for those misdeeds which she may have done.

Sefer Chasidim
* * * * *

Those that are aware of her difficult situation should pray to God that the woman should be well, and that the child should be born with good fortune.

Sefer Chasidim
* * * * *

A greater number of prayers (*tefillos*) should be said when unusual circumstances occur, i.e., that both (or all) children should remain well in a multiple birth, or in cases of possible (*ayin ha-ra*) bad fortune.

Sefer Chasidim
* * * * *

אלו סגולות ועצות
נמצאו בספרי קודש הנזכרים

צרכות הנשים ליזהר מאד במצות נדה, חלה, והדלקת הנר.

מבוסס על פי מסכת שבת פרק ב' משנה ו'

* * * * *

אשה שמקשה לילד לא ידברו בעון שעשתה וכן לחולה וכן מי שהלך
למלחמה, אלא לעצמו יחשוב הענין שישוב בתשובה כי עליונים מזכירים
דברי תחתונים.

ספר חסידים אות תפ"ו

* * * * *

אשה שיושבת על המשבר אם היא בחדר ובני אדם בבית יבקשו עליה רחמים
ועל הילד שיולד במזל טוב.

ספר חסידים אות תפ"ז

* * * * *

על כל דברים שאין רגיל להיות צריך להתחנן עליו כגון אשה שילדה תאומים
שיתקיימו שניהם ויותר צריך להתחנן אם ילדה שנים בתוך שנה מפני עין
הרע.

ספר חסידים אות תשצ"ב

* * * * *

When a woman enters her ninth month of pregnancy, she should take precautions every Friday to minimize, and if possible, eliminate anything that would cause desecration of the *Shabbos,* should it be necessary for her to give birth on *Shabbos.*

Sefer Chasidim

* * * * *

If a woman is having painful labor, someone should say the following *pasuk* (verse of scripture) to her . . . (see Hebrew on opposite page)

Taamei Ha-minhagim U'mekorai Ha-dinim

* * * * *

During the months of pregnancy, a woman should pray that the child should be born healthy and well. Prayer helps even in a case in which, God forbid, a bad decree was given by heaven to the mother or the child.

Shevet Mussar

* * * * *

אשה הרה וכבר הגיע חודש התשיעי להריונה, בערב שבת עם חשיכה יטמין
מים חמין כדי שאם תלד בליל שבת או בשבת הרי המים מזומנין ולא יחללו
שבת.

ספר חסידים אות תתנ"ה וגם הובא במגן אברהם אורח חיים סימן ש"ל סעיף קטן א' ועין
מסכת שבת דף קכ"ח: דכמה דאפשר לשנויי משנינן ומכל שכן מה דאפשר לעשות לפני שבת

* * * * *

סגולה למקשה לילד לומר לה זה הפסוק "וְיָרְדוּ כָל־עֲבָדֶיךָ אֵלֶּה אֵלַי וְהִשְׁתַּחֲווּ
לִי לֵאמֹר צֵא אַתָּה וְכָל־הָעָם אֲשֶׁר בְּרַגְלֶיךָ וְאַחֲרֵי כֵן אֵצֵא [וַיֵּצֵא
מֵעִם פַּרְעֹה בָּחֳרִי אָף]" (שמות יא:ח).

ספר טעמי המנהגים ומקורי הדינים (הובא בשם הספר ויכתב משה, פרשת בא בשם רבינו
בחיי) דף תקס"ז-תקס"ח

* * * * *

ובחדשי עיבורה תבקש רחמים שיהיה מתוקן באבריו ולא יהיה נפל שפיר
וסנדל או חולני. . . . שהתפלה מועלת לבטל הגזירה אף אם נגזר על הולד
איזה דבר מהנזכרים ולאה תוכיח שהפכה לדינה מזכר לנקבה כארז"ל.

ספר שבט מוסר פרק כ"ד

* * * * *

A woman, during pregnancy, should be extra careful of her actions, e.g. what she sees and hears, and even what she eats, because all of these have an effect on the unborn child. In order to have a good effect on the unborn child, she should try to accustom herself to good places, listen to *Torah* ideas, and try to gaze at Torah sages and *Tzaddikim* (righteous people).

Shevet Mussar

* * * * *

When a woman is having pain due to pregnancy, labor or delivery, she should have in mind that this pain should be an atonement for any sins which she may have committed.

Shevet Mussar

* * * * *

A *segulah* for women to have an easier delivery is to eat something for the sake of fulfilling the *mitzva* of *seudas Melave Malka* every *Motzaei Shabbos,* and at that time to express orally that "this is solely for the *mitzva* of the *seudas Melave Malka."*

Taamei Ha-minhagim U'mekorai Ha-dinim

* * * * *

גם תזהר שלא תכעוס בימי עיבורה . . . גם תהיה נזהרת בפרט בימי
עיבורה שלא תכנס במקומות של טומאה ובמקומות שיש שם ריח רע לפי
שהולד נוצר כפי ראות עיניה . . . אלא תשב בימי עיבורה במקומות קדושה
וטהרה בבתי כנסיות ומדרשות ותמיד לראות תלמידי חכמים חסידים ואנשי
מעשה ותשמע דברי תורה שהדברים נכנסים באזנה ומתקדש הולד בקרבה
שהאזן לגוף כקנקן לכלים כארז"ל שהולד שומע הכל ומבין.

ספר שבט מוסר פרק כ"ד

* * * * *

ואם יש בה שום עון תחשוב שמחול ומרוק אותו במה שנצטערה בכאב
החבלים.

ספר שבט מוסר פרק כ"ד

* * * * *

סגולה לנשים שלא יתקשו בלידתן הוא שיאכלו בכל מוצאי שבת קודש
איזה דבר לשם מצות סעודת מלוה מלכה. ואף גם יאמרו בפה מלא „לשם
מצות סעודת מלוה מלכה" ועל ידי זה ילדו בנקל בעזהשי"ת.

ספר טעמי המנהגים ומקורי הדינים (הובא בשם הרב הצדיק הקדוש רבי אלימלך זצוק"ל)
דף קס"ח

* * * * *

There is a custom, when a woman enters the ninth month of pregnancy, that the husband should perform the *mitzva* of opening the Holy Ark sometime during that month.

Avodas Ha-Kodesh

* * * * *

By the act of praising and thanking God, and also by learning Jewish Law and even more so if one can merit to reveal new insights in Jewish Law, through these actions the birth can come easier.

Likutei Aitzos

* * * * *

Supporting *Torah* by using one's assets to strengthen Torah sages can lighten the pain of childbirth.

Likutei Aitzos

* * * * *

A *segulah* for a woman who may have difficulty giving birth is to say Psalm 100—"מזמור לתודה„ (*Mizmor Le'sodah*). See Appendix, page 106.

Likutei Aitzos

* * * * *

ומנהג העיר שמי שנכנסה אשתו בחודש התשיעי לעיבורה נזהר לעשות החודש ההוא מצות פתיחת ההיכל והוא מנהג יפה ויש לו סמך על דרך אמת.

ספר עבודת הקודש—מורה באצבע פרק ג אות צ'

* * * * *

על ידי הלל והודאה להשי״ת וכן על ידי לימוד הלכות מכל שכן כשזוכין לחדש בהם על ידי זה באה הולדה בנקל.

ספר לקוטי עצות אות בנים פסוק י'

* * * * *

וכן על ידי תומכי אורייתא שמחזיקין בממונם את התלמידי חכמים על ידי זה ההולדה בנקל.

ספר לקוטי עצות אות בנים פסוק י'

* * * * *

סגולה למקשה לילד לומר מזמור לתודה [תהילים ק'] (נמצא בסוף הקונטרס) דף 106.

ספר לקוטי עצות אות בנים פסוק י״א

* * * * *

Another *segulah* for a woman who feels she may have difficulty giving birth is to do many acts of kindness, e.g. to give
more to charity, and to do deeds of bestowing kindness upon
others.

Likutei Aitzos

* * * * *

When a woman is having difficulty in childbirth, she
should be given snuff to inhale.

Taamei Ha-minhagim U'mekorai Ha-dinim

* * * * *

There is a custom for a pregnant woman to bite the tip of an
esrog.

Taamei Ha-minhagim U'mekorai Ha-dinim

* * * * *

A true *segulah* for all purposes is to be truly modest, to
give charity according to one's means, and to labor in the
study of *Torah* for its own sake.

Avodas Ha-Kodesh

* * * * *

גם סגולה למקשה לילד לעשות חסד הרבה דהיינו להרבות בצדקה וגמילות חסדים.

ספר לקוטי עצות אות בנים פסוק י"ב

* * * * *

למקשה לילד—תן לה בחוטמה שנופטאבאק (טבק להרחה), ואז יצאו הוולד עם השליא ממנה.

ספר טעמי המנהגים ומקורי הדינים (הובא בשם ספר סגולות ישראל) דף תקפ"א

* * * * *

טעם שהאשה נושכת את הפיטם של האתרוג מפני שאמרו ז"ל עץ שחטא בו אדם הראשון אתרוג היה, על כן נושכת את הפיטם כדי להראות כשם שאין לי שום הנאה בזאת הנשיכה, כך לא היה לי אז שום הנאה.

ספר טעמי המנהגים ומקורי הדינים דף תקכא (וגם ראיתי כאין זה בספר אלף המגן סימן תר"ס סעיף ו', בסוף ספר מטה אפרים.)

* * * * *

סגולה אמיתית לכל ענין הוא להיות עניו באמת מלב ונפש וליתן צדקה כפי מסת ידו ולעסוק בתורה לשמה וסימנך **עצ"ת יי היא תקום**, עצת ראשי תיבות **ע**נוה **צ**דקה **ת**ורה היא תקום. יי ברחמיו יזכנו להכיר מיעוט ערכנו ושפל מצבנו ולעסוק בתורתו תורת חיים.

ספר עבודת הקודש — כף אחת אות ל"ג

* * * * *

הלכות

* * * * * * *

LAWS

The *halachos* in the following section are based upon the *seforim* quoted in the footnotes. If the reader has any question, a competent Rabbi should be consulted.

הלכות שבת

* * * * * * * *

LAWS OF *SHABBOS*

INTRODUCTION

In the *Shulchan Aruch Orach Chayim* (330:1) it states that a woman who has given birth or is about to give birth is considered a sick person who is in danger, and it is permissible to desecrate the *Shabbos* on her behalf. **It is necessary to keep in mind that one should do whatever can be done before *Shabbos* (e.g. setting aside money for a taxi) in order to minimize the amount of *Chilul Shabbos*.** It is permissible to call a midwife (or doctor) for her, and it is permissible to light a candle (or put on a light) on *Shabbos* even for a blind woman if this will reassure her.[1] However, whenever possible, it is best to do whatever *melacha* needs to be done in an unusual manner (in order that it should not be considered a *melacha d'Oraysa*). For example, if the woman about to give birth needs something [which needs to be carried from one domain to another on *Shabbos*] it can be

---

[1] משנה ברורה שם.

77

brought to her hanging on her friend's hair, instead of carrying it by hand.[2]

It was said above that one is permitted to desecrate the *Shabbos* in a case of danger to life. The same rule applies even if there is only a remote possibility that there is an actual danger to life.[3] As far as determining if there is a question of danger to one's life, any responsible person is considered competent enough to make this decision.[4]

Also, it was stated previously that actions ordinarily not permitted on *Shabbos* should be done not in the usual manner. This is to be done only as long as by using a different manner to do something, the rescue would not be delayed. If there is even a possibility of any delay, then we do everything necessary for the person in need, in the normal manner.[5]

One should not hesitate or delay in any way helping the person whose life is endangered, for it is not only permitted to desecrate the *Shabbos* for that person, but it is regarded a great *mitzva*. If one is afraid to desecrate the *Shabbos* until he asks a *Shailah* at a time of danger to life, he is considered a murderer.[6]

Also, if the one whose life is in danger does not want anyone to desecrate the *Shabbos* for him, we are not permitted to heed his request, and if necessary, we are obligated to force the ill person to do whatever is necessary. If the person in danger says he needs something, even if the doctor says it is not necessary,

² משנה ברורה שם.

³ רמב"ם הלכות שבת פרק ב' הלכה א', ושלחן ערוך אורח חיים סימן שכ"ט סעיף ג'.

⁴ שלחן ערוך אורח חיים סימן שכ"ח סעיף י'.

⁵ שלחן ערוך אורח חיים סימן שכ"ח סעיף י"ב בהג"ה.

⁶ שלחן ערוך אורח חיים סימן שכ"ח סעיף ב' ובמשנה ברורה סעיף קטן י'.

we listen to the *choleh* and we are *mechalel* the *Shabbos* for him. This is so unless the doctor says that this procedure is dangerous to the patient's condition.[7]

Please note:

In a situation where it is inevitable that a *melacha* will be done, if possible **one should not assist** the person that is actually doing the *melacha*. For example, if a woman is being finger-printed after childbirth, she should leave her hand limp and not assist in this *melacha*. Or if her temperature is to be taken on *Shabbos* with a digital thermometer she should let the nurse put it under her tongue and also take it out.

TELEPHONING THE DOCTOR

A woman is permitted to call her doctor by telephone on *Shabbos* even before she is considered a *yoledes* (refer to "Laws when a Woman is Considered a *Niddah*" pg. 92). This is permitted if she feels that she needs the doctor's immediate advice and instructions. This also applies if serious bleeding occurs during her pregnancy, or when any question of possible danger either to the woman or to the fetus has to be clarified.[8]

When telephoning on *Shabbos* in a case of necessity, the receiver, where possible, should preferably be knocked off the hook in an unusual way (e.g. with one's elbow).

Dialing the number should also not to be done normally (e.g. it should be done with the tip of a spoon). If one has a phone with a memory, he should program whatever numbers might be necessary before *Shabbos* in order to minimize the number of buttons that will have to be pressed on *Shabbos*.

If more than one call must be made, or if the doctor has to call back, then the receiver may be hung up after the last call is made. If no more calls have to be made, and no more calls have to come in, the receiver should not be hung up, but left off the hook.

[8] סימן ש"ל במשנה ברורה סעיף קטן ט'.

GOING TO THE HOSPITAL ON *SHABBOS*

As was mentioned above, a person must think ahead, and take care of whatever he can do for the *choleh* before *Shabbos,* in order to minimize the amount of *melacha* done on *Shabbos.* A woman at any time in her ninth month may have to go to the hospital on *Shabbos.* Therefore, every Friday in the ninth month she should do whatever she can to minimize any *chilul Shabbos.* This includes setting aside money for a taxi, or if possible making arrangements with a taxi service to pay them before or after *Shabbos.* Arrangements should also be made in advance for taking care of the children in the family on *Shabbos.*[9]

It is permissible for the husband, mother, or someone else to accompany the woman about to give birth to the hospital, if their being there will make her more relaxed or confident.[10]

It is preferable that nothing be taken along to the hospital on *Shabbos,* but whatever is needed should be brought after *Shabbos.* However, if there is something that is essential to assist the woman, or to prevent her from getting agitated, it can be brought to the hospital on *Shabbos.* [note: Wine for *Kiddush* or a *Siddur* for *davening* do not fall into the category of what can be brought on *Shabbos.*]

---

[9] סימן ש"ל במשנה ברורה סעיף קטן א'.

[10] אגרות חזון איש חלק א' סימן קמ"א; אגרות משה אורח חיים חלק א' סימן קל"ב; שמירת שבת כהלכתה פרק מ' סעיף ע'.

It is most advisable to go to the hospital in a car driven by a gentile, and if possible, to make an arrangement with the taxi so as not to pay them on *Shabbos*.[11] If it is necessary to pay them on *Shabbos,* it is preferable to tell the gentile to come into the house and take the money that was set aside for this purpose before *Shabbos*. If this is not possible, then one should take the least amount of bills possible (e.g. one twenty dollar bill instead of a ten and a five dollar bill) and carry them out in an unusual manner (e.g. in one's shoe).

Please note that calling on a gentile to do *melacha*, or doing *melacha* in an unusual manner should only be done if this will not cause any danger to the life of the mother or child. However, if calling a gentile or doing things in an unusual way will delay matters to the point of danger, then it is a *mitzva* for the people involved to do whatever needs to be done as quickly as possible in the usual way.[12]

If it is not possible to obtain a gentile to drive the person(s) to the hospital, the next best thing is to get a car operated by a Jew. In such a case, the passengers are obligated to see that the minimum amount of *chilul Shabbos* is done by the driver. In a case where the driver will surely not listen to what he is told, there is no purpose in trying to help him minimize the *chilul Shabbos*. However, if the passengers can influence the driver, the guidelines that apply when one is forced to take his own car on *Shabbos* should be followed.

11 שמירת שבת כהלכתה שם והכל מבוסס על שלחן ערוך אורח חיים סימן שכ"ח סעיף ד';
משנה ברורה סעיף קטן י"ד; שער הציון י"א, וביאור הלכה ד"ה כל.
12 שלחן ערוך אורח חיים סימן שכ"ח סעיף י"ב בהג"ה.

If one cannot make any arrangements with a taxi service, and he is forced to take his own car on *Shabbos*, the following general rules should be observed:

(1) If it is possible to leave the car door unlocked and the key in the ignition before *Shabbos* to prevent carrying on *Shabbos*, it would be preferred. If this is not possible, then the key should be carried out to the car not in the regular way (e.g. it should be carried in one's shoe). After the door is opened, the key should again be carried into the car in an unusual manner (e.g. return it to one's shoe).

(2) If the light in the car goes on as soon as the door is opened, one is still permitted to enter. However, if something can be done to keep the lights on it is advisable (even if this will later drain the battery). If keeping on the lights will make driving more difficult or dangerous (at night, perhaps) then this should not be done. If it is impossible after first opening the door to keep the lights on, then only one door should be opened (the passenger's side) and both the husband and wife should enter through there.

(3) Care should be taken not to make any unnecessary stops or changes in gear (e.g. backing up) because this will cause lights to go on.

(4) If one is traveling at night, it is permissible to put on the headlights. However, it is forbidden at the end of the ride to close the headlights, even if the battery will become drained, or even if the driver will receive a ticket for not doing so.

(5) One should take the shortest route to the hospital. If the woman's doctor is in a hospital a further distance away, and there is a closer hospital, one is not obligated to go to a nearer hospital.

(6) Upon arriving at the hospital one should park his car at the first available space, even if this means getting a ticket (e.g. where "doctors only" park). One should not ride around to search for a suitable parking space. Yet, one should be careful not to park his car in a place that will endanger other people (e.g. blocking the entrance of the hospital).

(7) Upon arrival at the hospital, one should locate a gentile to turn off the engine. If there is no gentile available one should look for a minor—under the age of *Bar* or *Bas Mitzvah*. If this is also impossible, then one may turn off the engine himself, as long as this action does not also shut off the lights.[13]

---

[13] כללים אלו מספר שמירת שבת כהלכתה פרק מ'.

IN THE HOSPITAL

If a woman in active labor comes to the hospital and must sign a paper, it is permissible. If possible, it is preferable to ask a gentile to fill out the forms. However, many hospitals are more flexible, and this could be taken care of before or after *Shabbos,* or by the doctor's intervention.[14]

IF THE WOMAN IS NOT
READY TO DELIVER
(False Alarm)

If after being examined, it is ascertained that it is not necessary for the woman to stay in the hospital, and that she will not be admitted, the most desirable thing to do is for that couple to stay until *Shabbos* is over, and to go home after *Shabbos*. If this is not possible (e.g. the woman must have a place to lie down), then, since the woman is considered a sick person not in danger, a gentile can drive her home. However, the husband, or whoever accompanied her to the hospital must remain until *Shabbos* is over, just as he must do when his wife does actually give birth on a *Shabbos*.[15]

14 שלחן ערוך אורח חיים סימן שכ"ח סעיף י"ז ובמשנה ברורה סעיף קטן מ"ז.

15 שלחן ערוך אורח חיים סימן שכ"ח סעיף י"ז, ובמשנה ברורה סעיף קטן מ"ז.

AFTER DELIVERY
(OR MISCARRIAGE)[16]

THE FIRST THREE DAYS

From the time a woman gives birth until 72 hours thereafter (3 days), she is considered a sick person whose life is in danger. Therefore anything that she needs to improve her condition may be done.[17] Whenever possible it is preferable to do *melacha* on *Shabbos* by means of a gentile or a minor. However, if such is not available or if their assistance will not be enough, then it is a *mitzva* to perform whatever is needed by a Jewish adult. (e.g. If the electric bed has to be moved up or down, to improve her condition (not merely for comfort), or a light has to be turned on or off, it may be done, if needed, even by a Jewish adult if a non-Jew or a minor is not available.)[18] If something is needed for comfort only and involves a *melacha d'Oraysa,* a gentile should be asked to perform the act.[19]

THE FOURTH DAY UNTIL THE SEVENTH DAY

From 72 hours after having given birth until 168 hours thereafter (7 days), a woman is considered (under normal circumstances) a sick person not in danger. At this time, *melacha* can be done for her on *Shabbos* only through a gentile, not through a Jew. It is then permitted to ask a gentile directly to do

16 ביאור הלכה סימן תרי"ז ד"ה „יולדת" בשם שדי חמד.
17 שלחן ערוך אורח חיים סימן ש"ל סעיף ד'.
18 שלחן ערוך אורח חיים סימן שכ"ח סעיף ב', י"א, י"ב, י"ג, וגו'.
19 משנה ברורה סימן שכ"ח סעיף קטן י"ד ובביאור הלכה שם.

something that involves a *melacha d'Oraysa* (e.g. turning on a light).[20]

USING A BREAST PUMP

Extracting milk from one's breast is a *melacha d'Oraysa* if the milk is going to be used. However, if the milk is extracted in order to alleviate the mother's pain, and it will go to waste, then it is permitted. Therefore, using a breast pump is permitted on *Shabbos* for the purpose of alleviating pain, but care must be taken that the milk extracted should not be used. The best thing to do is to place something (not *muktzah*) in the breast pump (e.g. vinegar) that would make the milk unfit to drink.

If this is not possible, then the breast pump should be emptied out very often to make sure that not more than 2 ounces accumulate at one time.[21]

[20] שם סימן שכ"ח סעיף י"ז ובמשנה ברורה.

[21] סימן ש"ל סעיף ח', ובמשנה ברורה סעיף קטן ס'; שמירת שבת כהלכתה פרק ל"ו אות כ'.

הדלקת הנרות

* * * * * * * *

LIGHTING CANDLES ON *SHABBOS*
OR *YOM TOV*

While the woman is in the hospital, or even if she is home but she is unable to light the *Shabbos* or *Yom Tov* candles, her husband can light them for her.[22]

If the husband lights the candles at home, when his wife is in the hospital, but she is given permission to light candles there, then she should also light the candles.[23]

If both she and her husband were unable to light the candles, (e.g. they both came to the hospital immediately before *Shabbos*), she is not obligated to add an extra candle on *Shabbos* or *Yom Tov* for the rest of her life.

The law of adding one additional candle only applies if the woman was once negligent, and did not light candles (e.g. if she always lit two candles, from now on she must light three candles for *Shabbos* or *Yom Tov*).[24]

[22] משנה ברורה סימן רס"ג סעיף קטן י"א.
[23] שם במשנה ברורה סעיף קטן ל"ח.
[24] סימן רס"ג סעיף א' ובהג"ה, ובמשנה ברורה שם סעיף קטן ז'.

הלכות נדה

* * * * * * * *

LAWS OF *NIDDAH*

INTERNAL EXAMINATIONS DURING PREGNANCY

After a woman has not seen her period for 3 months because of her pregnant condition, she may consider herself permissible without any internal examinations.[25]

Before 3 months time has elapsed, however, even if it is visible that she is expecting, and even if it was determined through reliable tests that she is pregnant, a woman is still not considered as if her period has stopped, and she is required to separate from her husband, at the time of her expected *vest*. She is also required to make the necessary internal examinations at the time of her expected *vest*.[26]

[25] שלחן ערוך יורה דעה סימן קפ״ט סעיף ל״ג, סימן קפ״ד סעיף ז׳, ועיין גם בסימן ק״צ סעיף נ״ב.

[26] שאלות ותשובות ר׳ עקיבא איגר סימן קכ״ח; אבני נזר סימן רל״ח; פרדס רימונים סימן קפ״ד, במקשה זהב סעיף קטן י׳; אגרות משה יורה דעה חלק ג׳ סימן נ״ב; חזקת טהרה סימן קפ״ט סעיף ל״ד; בדרך ישרה אות ל״ג.

WHAT ARE A WOMAN'S EXPECTED *VESTS* DURING THIS THREE MONTH PERIOD OF TIME

I. A woman who has an established *vest*

1. If the *vest* is established to come after an exact same number of days every month (e.g. every 35 days), and during the same part of the day (e.g. either during the night time or daytime) then a woman is only required to separate from her husband, and also make an internal examination on the 35th day, and she need not make any more on any other days.

2. If the *vest* is established to come on a certain day each month (note: when we say month, we refer to the **Hebrew** month), then during the 3 month period she must keep this day as her anticipated *vest,* by separating from her husband and making internal examinations on that day. (e.g. If the *vest* always comes on the 5th of the month, then for the next 3 months, the 5th day is her expected *vest*.)

II. A woman who does not have an established *vest*

1. During the first month of pregnancy, a woman must observe all the days which are required, as follows:
   (a) the interval of days from the last period plus
   (b) the 30th day and
   (c) the 31st day since the last period. (e.g. If the interval between the last 2 periods was 27 days, then on the 27th, 30th and 31st day, a woman must observe these days as days of her expected *vest*.)

2. During the remainder of the 3 months no examinations are required.[27]

[27] כמבואר ביורה דעה סימן קפ"ד, קפ"ט.

EXAMINATIONS BY A DOCTOR
DURING THE TIME A WOMAN IS NOT SEEING BLOOD

1. If the doctor made the examination with his finger, then there is no reason to suspect that the woman saw blood, and she does not have to make an internal examination.[28]

2. **If the doctor uses an instrument**:

(a) If the doctor says the instrument went as far as her uterus (מקור), she is considered as if she saw blood, even if she makes a *bedika* and does not find any. She must also wait five days if her husband was permitted to her and count seven clean days.

(b) If the doctor says that he did not go into her uterus, then she should make a *bedika* after his examination, and if she does not see any blood, she is permitted to be with her husband.

(c) If the doctor says that he did not go into the uterus, but he says that he did wound her, and there is blood from the injury (not from the מקור), then even if the doctor is not an observant Jew, we can believe him, and she is permitted to her husband.[29]

(d) A pap smear presents no problems.[30]

Note: A woman should always get as many facts as possible from the doctor. Where there is any doubt she should ask a *Shailah*.

28 בינת אדם אות כ"ג; שאלות ותשובות חתם סופר סימן קע"ט; דרכי תשובה סימן קצ"ד סעיף קטן י"ט; ועוד.

29 אגרות משה יורה דעה חלק א' סימן פ"ג, צ"ה; שאלות ותשובות מנחת יצחק חלק ג' סימן פ"ד.

30 מפי רופאים נאמנים, וגם כל הרבנים כך פוסקים.

WHEN DOES A WOMAN THAT IS IN LABOR
BECOME A *NIDDAH*

If one of the following occurs, then a woman has to suspect that she is a *niddah*:

1. Her pains are so severe that she feels she must sit or lie down on a bed ready for delivery.

2. She is unable to walk without assistance.

3. Her water broke and any trace of blood is noticed.[31]

Note: If the woman is a *niddah* and needs assistance, and only her husband can assist her, then he is permitted.

סדרי טהרה סימן קצ"ד סעיף קטן כ"ה; אגרות משה יורה דעה חלק ב' סימן ע"ה. [31]

CAN A HUSBAND BE WITH HIS WIFE IN THE LABOR AND DELIVERY ROOM

The husband may remain in the labor and delivery room to assist and to give encouragement and comfort to his wife.

However, *he must be very careful* not to look at any places that are usually covered. He should be aware that his wife is a *niddah* and all the laws of separation apply. He is also strictly forbidden to look at the place where the baby is coming out. It is also forbidden even if he looks at a mirror which focuses on the baby coming out.[32]

THIS VIEW IS BASED SOLELY UPON *HALACHA*. HOWEVER, THERE ARE MANY OPINIONS THAT IN ORDER TO COMPLY FULLY WITH THE LAWS OF *TZNIUS*, THE HUSBAND SHOULD NOT BE PRESENT IN THE DELIVERY ROOM.

[32] אגרות משה יורה דעה חלק ב' סימן ע"ה.

הלכות תענית

* * * * * * * *

LAWS OF FASTING

Please refer to the comments at the end of this section p. 97.

FASTING DURING PREGNANCY
OR FOR NURSING WOMEN

1. **צום גדליה, עשרה בטבת, תענית אסתר, י"ז תמוז**—*Tzom Gedaliah, Asarah B'Teves, Taanis Esther, Shive'ah Asar B'Tammuz*

During these minor fasts, if a woman who is pregnant or nursing feels weak, she is not required to fast.[33] [d]

2. **תשעה באב**—*Tisha B'Av*

A woman, pregnant or nursing, is required to fast, and complete the fast like other healthy people.[a,b]

However, when *Tisha B'Av* falls out on *Shabbos,* and is postponed till Sunday, then if she feels weak, she is permitted to eat after a half-hour past midday.[34] [c]

3. **יום כפור**—*Yom Kippur*

As long as a pregnant or nursing woman is not in any danger, she is required to fast the complete fast.[35] [a,b,d]

---

[33] שלחן ערוך אורח חיים סימן תק"ן בהג"ה, וגם במשנה ברורה שם סעיף קטן ב', ה'.

[34] שערי תשובה סימן תקנ"ה סעיף קטן ב' בשם שבות יעקב.

[35] שלחן ערוך אורח חיים סימן תרי"ז סעיף א', ועיין שם בביאור הלכה ד"ה עוברות.

94

FASTING FOR A WOMAN WHO HAS JUST GIVEN BIRTH OR HAS JUST HAD A MISCARRIAGE[36]

I. During the first three days[f]

During this time period it is forbidden for a woman to fast even on *Yom Kippur* and even if she says that she feels well enough to fast.[37]

II. After three days until seven days

1. If the woman feels that she can fast, but the doctor says that she should not, due to the harm it may cause her or the child, then she must eat even on *Yom Kippur*,[e] and surely on the other fasts.[38]

2. If the woman feels that she cannot fast, then even if the doctor says that she can fast, she still should eat,[e] even on *Yom Kippur*.[39]

3. If the doctor did not tell her that she may fast, and she is not sure if she is strong enough, then she should eat even on *Yom Kippur*.[40] [e]

---

[36] ביאור הלכה סימן תרי"ז ד"ה יולדת בשם שדי חמד.

[37] שלחן ערוך אורח חיים סימן תרי"ז סעיף ד'; משנה ברורה סעיף קטן י'.

[38] שלחן ערוך שם; משנה ברורה סעיף קטן י"א.

[39] שם.

[40] שם.

III. After seven days until thirty days

During this time period she has the *din* of a sick person who is not in danger, and (a) is obligated to fast on *Yom Kippur*[41a] and (b) on *Tisha B'Av*. She is not obligated to complete the fast but need only fast a few hours. However, if she feels strong and is confident that the fast will not affect her health then she should fast the entire day.[42] (c) *Tzom Gedaliah, Asarah B'Teves, Taanis Esther, Shive'ah Asar B'Tammuz* she may eat if she feels weak.[43]

IV. After thirty days

After thirty days, she no longer has the *din* of a woman who has given birth but has the *din* of a regular person.[44]

---

[41] שם משנה ברורה סעיף קטן י"ב.

[42] קיצור שלחן ערוך סימן קכ"ד סעיף ו'. ועיין שלחן ערוך אורח חיים סימן תקנ"ד סעיף ו' בהגה"ה.

[43] קיצור שלחן ערוך סימן קכ"ד מבוסס על דברי רמ"א (תקנ"ד סעיף ו') ודברי הט"ז (שם סעיף קטן ד'), ועיין גם בערוך השלחן (שם סעיף ז').

[44] קיצור שלחן ערוך סימן קכ"ד סעיף ו'. ועיין שלחן ערוך אורח חיים סימן תקנ"ד סעיף ו' בהגה"ה.

NOTES:

a. Whenever we say that a person must fast, of course this does not hold true if there is a danger to the life of that person (or for a nursing woman—a danger to the baby's life) If there is any danger, she is forbidden to fast.[45]

b. If a nursing woman feels well enough to fast, but by fasting, her nursing child will not have enough to eat, then she is obligated not to fast.

c. *Mincha G'dola*—½ hour after midday (does not mean 12:30 PM). The time varies according to the area. It can be checked by consulting a *Rav*.

d. When it is permissible for a person to eat, he should not eat or drink more than necessary to keep himself (and for a nursing woman—the child) healthy.[46]

e. She should eat only small amounts of food at a time.[47]

f. When we refer to a day we mean 24 hours. Therefore, 3 days equals a full 72 hours, and seven days is a full 168 hours after birth.[48]

[45] דעת תורה סימן תק"ן.

[46] שלחן ערוך אורח חיים סימן תקנ"ד סעיף ה'.

[47] שלחן ערוך אורח חיים סימן תרי"ז; משנה ברורה סעיף קטן א'; סימן תרי"ח סעיף ז', ח'.

[48] שלחן ערוך אורח חיים תרי"ח; משנה ברורה סעיף קטן י"ג.

כהן בבית החולים
* * * * * * *
KOHEN IN A HOSPITAL

In a case of necessity, it is permitted for a *kohen* to visit his wife or relative who is in the hospital, but he should only stay as long as he has to.

Note: If there is any actual problem of a Jewish corpse in the hospital that could cause the *Kohen* to become *Tamay*, then the *Kohen* is not permitted to go in at all.[49]

[49] אגרות משה יורה דעה חלק ב׳ סימן קס״ו.

ברכת הודאה

* * * * * * * *

BLESSINGS UPON THE BIRTH
OF A CHILD

The following *Halachos* (Jewish Laws) are a general summary of the requirements for making a *brocha* (blessing)* upon the birth of a child. These *halachos* are for normal conditions. Please note, however, that the law may differ in certain unusual circumstances (e.g. God forbid the death of the parents, or if the newborn's life is in danger). In cases such as these, a competent Rabbi should be consulted.

BIRTH OF A BOY

When a boy is born, the father of the child should make the *brocha* הטוב והמטיב (*Ha-tov Ve-ha-maytiv*).[50] This *brocha* can be said even if he did not yet see his new son,[51] but only **hears** the news. However, if he will shortly be seeing his son, he can wait to make the *brocha* at that time, since his joy will be greater then. If he did not make the *brocha* then, he can still make the *brocha* at a later time, as soon as possible, before the feeling of joy of the new birth wanes.[52]

* See Appendix for exact wording of blessings, page 107.

---

[50] מחבר סימן רכ"ג סעיף א'.

[51] משנה ברורה סימן רכ"ג סעיף קטן א'.

[52] שם סעיף קטן ג' ועיין בסעיף קטן ט"ו.

99

BIRTH OF A GIRL

When a girl is born, the *brocha* made is שהחיינו (*she'he'-cheyanu*). (Some *Poskim* hold that no *brocha* is made.[53]) This *brocha* must be said by the father upon **seeing** his newborn daughter for the first time.[54] If one did not say the *brocha* then, he can say it as long as the feeling of joy of the new birth did not wane. (This time period is approximately one week.[55])

MULTIPLE BIRTH

When both children born are boys then only one *brocha* of הטוב והמטיב (*Ha-tov Ve-ha-maytiv*) can be made[56] (see section on **Birth of a Boy**). If they are both girls, then one *brocha* of שהחיינו (*she'he'cheyanu*) can be made when **seeing** both of them together[57] (see section on **Birth of a Girl**). In the case of a boy and girl, the father can make one *brocha* of הטוב והמטיב (*Ha-tov Ve-ha-maytiv*) when **seeing** them together.[58]

---

[53] ערוך השלחן סימן רכ"ג סעיף א'.

[54] משנה ברורה סימן רכ"ג סעיף קטן ב'.

[55] כך שמעתי מפי הגאון ר' משה פיינשטיין זצ"ל.

[56] משנה ברורה סימן רכב סעיף קטן ב'.

[57] שם.

[58] כך שמעתי מפי הגאון ר' משה פיינשטיין זצ"ל.

OBLIGATION OF THE MOTHER

A woman is also obligated to make these *brochos,* but she cannot do so until she has been properly washed, and is in the proper state of mind to fully appreciate the *simcha.*[59]

If, when her husband comes to see his son for the first time, she hasn't yet made the *brocha* of הטוב והמטיב (*Ha-tov Ve-ha-maytiv*), he can exempt her (since this is a *brocha* that is made to acknowledge the goodness of *Hashem* to more than one person).[60] However, they are not required to wait for the express purpose that the husband exempt his wife.[61] In the case of the *brocha* שהחיינו (*She'he'cheyanu*) after the birth of a girl, the husband and wife should make separate *brochos.*[62]

Now „אסור לו לאדם שיהנה מן העולם הזה בלא ברכה." (ברכות לה.) that you have made the proper *brocha,* may you be worthy of much *yiddishe nachas* from your new baby.

---

[59] שם.

[60] שם.

[61] שם.

[62] שם ועיין משנה ברורה סימן ח' סעיף קטן י"ד.

חיוב הבעל לעלות לתורה

* * * * * * * *

OBLIGATION OF THE HUSBAND TO BE CALLED UP TO THE *TORAH*

When one's wife is well enough to go to *shule* on the *Shabbos* after she has given birth, then the husband, at that time is obligated to be called up to the *Torah*. However, if she does not come to *shule*, then the husband is not obligated to be called up to the *Torah*. If the wife does not come to *shule*, by the 40th day after the birth (or miscarriage) of a boy or the 80th day after the birth (or miscarriage) of a girl, the husband is obligated to be called up to the *Torah*.[63]

---

[63] ביאור הלכה סימן קל"ז ד"ה בשבת.

ברכת הגומל

* * * * * * * *

THANKSGIVING BLESSING

There are various customs as to whether the thanksgiving blessing is to be said on the occasion of the birth of a child. It is also questionable if the woman makes this blessing, or her husband makes it for her. In this matter, one should follow their family custom. If there is any question, a competent *Rav* should be consulted.[64]

---

[64] ביאור הלכה סימן רי״ט סעיף קטן י״ז.

APPENDIX

תפילת מזמור לתודה

(תהלים ק')

מִזְמוֹר לְתוֹדָה, הָרִיעוּ לַיי כָּל־הָאָרֶץ: עִבְדוּ אֶת יי בְּשִׂמְחָה, בְּאוּ לְפָנָיו בִּרְנָנָה: דְעוּ כִּי יי הוּא אֱלֹהִים, הוּא עָשָׂנוּ, וְלוֹ אֲנַחְנוּ עַמוֹ, וְצֹאן מַרְעִיתוֹ: בְּאוּ שְׁעָרָיו בְּתוֹדָה, חֲצֵרוֹתָיו בִּתְהִלָּה, הוֹדוּ לוֹ בָּרְכוּ שְׁמוֹ: כִּי טוֹב יי, לְעוֹלָם חַסְדּוֹ, וְעַד דֹּר וָדֹר אֱמוּנָתוֹ:

* * * * *

Mizmor L'Sodah

Psalm 100

A psalm of thanksgiving. Call out to God, all the earth. Serve God with gladness: come before His presence with singing. Know that the Lord He is God: it is He who made us, and we belong to Him; we are His people and the sheep of His pasture. Enter into His gates with thanksgiving and into His courts with praise: be thankful to Him, and bless His name.For the Lord is good; His love endures forever; and His faithfulness extends to all generations.

**These are the *brochos* which were discussed
in the *Halacha* section.**

She'he'cheyanu Benediction—ברכת שהחיינו

בָּרוּךְ אַתָּה יי אֱלֹהֵינוּ מֶלֶךְ הָעוֹלָם שֶׁהֶחֱיָינוּ וְקִיְּמָנוּ וְהִגִּיעָנוּ לַזְּמַן הַזֶּה.

Boruch atoh Adonoy Elohaynu Melech ha-olam, she-he-cheyanu ve-kiy-manu, ve-higiyanu lazman ha-zeh.

Blessed be You, O God, our God, King of the universe, who has kept us in life, and sustained and enabled us to reach this time.

Ha-tov Ve-ha-maytiv Benediction—ברכת הטוב והמטיב

בָּרוּךְ אַתָּה יי אֱלֹהֵינוּ מֶלֶךְ הָעוֹלָם הַטּוֹב וְהַמֵּטִיב.

Boruch atoh Adonoy Elohaynu Melech ha-olam, Ha-tov ve-ha-maytiv.

Blessed be You, O God, our God, King of the universe, who is good and does good.

GLOSSARY

Aitzos — suggestions; advice

Aleph — first letter of the Hebrew alphabet

Asarah BeTeves — tenth of Teves which commemorates the day when the Babylonians began their siege of Jerusalem.

Av — one of the Hebrew months of the year.

Ayin — sixteenth letter of the Hebrew alphabet

Ayin Ha-ra — literally an evil eye; to wish ill fortune on one's fellow man

B'mazel Tov — with good fortune

Bais — second letter of the Hebrew alphabet

Bais Din — Rabbinical court

Bar mitzva — the initiation of a boy at the age of thirteen into the Jewish religious community.

Bas mitzva — the initiation of a girl at the age of twelve into the Jewish religious community.

Bedika — examination

Ben — son of

Berachos — a tractate of the *Talmud*

Brocha (Brochos) — blessing(s) or benedictions(s) recited before partaking of food and drink, before performing most *mitzvos,* and on many other occasions.

Chachmei Ashkenaz — the Rabbinical leaders of Ashkenaz; a term used to designate the concentration of Jews in northern France, Germany and Eastern Europe, beginning in the 10th century.

Chachmei S'fard — Rabbinical leaders of Jews living in the Iberian peninsula between the 10th and 15th centuries. S'fard was later used as a term for all Jews living in the Mediterranean region.

Challah — literally a cake, obligation to separate a portion of the dough before the remainder is baked into bread

Chassidic—Chassidism — religious movement founded by Rabbi Yisroel Baal Shem Tov in the first half of the 18th century.

Chava — Eve, the first woman created

Chazal — our sages of blessed memory; a statement of the sages.

Ches — eighth letter of the Hebrew alphabet

Chilul Shabbos — desecrating or literally making plain the Holy *Shabbos*

Choleh — a sick person
Chulin — a tractate of the *Talmud*
Dalet — fourth letter of the Hebrew alphabet
Davening — praying
Dayyan — judge
Din(im) — law(s)
Dovid Hamelech — King David
Erechin — a tractate of the *Talmud*
Eretz Yisroel — the land of Israel
Eruvin — a tractate of the *Talmud*
Esther Raba — *Midrash* on the Book of Esther
Gemara — section of *Talmud* which explains the *Mishna*
G'zerah — a heavenly decree
Ha-Kadosh Boruch Hu — the Holy One, blessed be He
Hakoras Ha-tov — appreciation
Ha-Koton — literally means "the small one," denoting modesty
Halacha (Halachos) — a Jewish law, rule or regulation
Halachist — a *Torah* scholar who is an authority in Jewish Law
Harav Ha-gaon — literally, the Rabbi, the genius
Hashem — literally "the name" referring to God whose holy name we
    do not pronounce in vain
Ha-Tov Ve-ha-maytiv — blessing said upon hearing good tidings that
    involve two or more people
Hay — fifth letter of the Hebrew alphabet
Kabbalah — literally means reception; oral tradition. Especially used
    to designate mystical teachings of Judaism.
Kabbalist — a *Torah* scholar who is well versed in *Kabbalah*.
Kiddush — prayer recited over wine on the *Shabbos* or *Yom Tov*
Kislev — one of the Hebrew months of the year
Kohen — priest
Koof — nineteenth letter of the Hebrew alphabet
Lamed — twelfth letter of the Hebrew alphabet
La-M'natzai'ach Mizmor LeDovid — Psalm 20
Loshon Hora — a derogatory or harmful statement; slander, evil talk
Maggid — speaker, preacher
MarCheshvan — one of the Hebrew months of the year

Mashgiach Ruchani — spiritual supervisor in a yeshiva

Mechalel — to desecrate

Melacha (Melachos) — one of the 39 categories of work forbidden on *Shabbos*

Melacha D'Oraysa — a *melacha* forbidden based on a Torah principle

Melave Malka — literally, escorting the (Sabbath) queen; a meal eaten on *Motzai Shabbos*

Midrash — the moral and philosophical teachings of the *Torah*, its homiletical exposition

Mikvah — a gathering of water in a structure conforming to the laws of ritual immersion

Mincha G'dola — ½ hour after midday (does not mean 12:30 p.m.). The time varies according to the area. It can be checked by consulting a *Rav*.

Mishlei — the book of Proverbs written by King Shlomo (Solomon)

Mishnah — earliest codification of Jewish Oral Law

Mishnah B'rurah — A comprehensive commentary on *Shulchan Aruch, Orach Chayim* written by Rav Yisrael Meir Ha-Kohen (The Chofetz Chaim)

Mitzva—(Mitzvos) — A positive or negative commandment. Any one of the 613 *Torah*-given precepts, and one of the later added Rabbinical Commandments

Mizmor L'sodah — Psalm 100; also part of the morning services

Motzaei Shabbos — Saturday night after the Sabbath

Moreh Tzedek — *halachic* authority

Muktzah — literally, set apart—items which are *muktzah* may not be moved or eaten

Nachas — joy, comfort

Niddah — a woman who has an issue of any amount of blood from her uterus, and has not yet undergone the prescribed seven clean days, and immersion in a *mikvah*.

Nikud — vowelization of Hebrew words

Nun — fourteenth letter of the Hebrew alphabet

Orach Chayim — the first of the four sections of *Shulchan Aruch* that deals with every day laws

Pasuk — verse of scripture

Poskim — *halachic* authorities

R'chilus — relating to someone that another person said or did something against him

Rabbeim — *Torah* teachers

Rabbeinu — literally our Rabbi, teacher

Raish — twentieth letter of the Hebrew alphabet

Rav — Rabbi

Rosh Chodesh — literally, the new moon; the first day of each month celebrated as a quasi-festival

Rosh(ei) Ha-Yeshiva — dean(s) of *Torah* academy

Sefer (Sefarim) — book(s)

Segulah (Segulos) — spiritual remedy; talisman; treasure

Seudas — the meal of

Shabbos — the Sabbath; the day of rest (from sundown Friday eve till the stars come out on Saturday night); a tractate of the *Talmud*

Shailah — a question in *Halacha*

She'he'cheyanu — blessing said in praise for special occasions

She'lo Ke'derech Ha-teva — literally, not in the way of nature; unusual

Shive'ah Asar B'Tammuz — seventeenth day of the month of *Tammuz*; a fast day which commemorates the day when the Babylonian army made the first breach in the wall of Jerusalem during the siege then.

Shulchan Aruch — compilation of practical *Torah* laws

Shule — synagogue

Siddur — prayer book

Simcha — rejoicing

Sin — twenty-first Hebrew letter of the Hebrew alphabet

Sivan — one of the Hebrew months of the year.

S'micha — the term used for the process of ordaining a Rabbi

Suv — twenty second letter of the Hebrew alphabet

Taanis Esther — Fast of Esther which commemorates the time when the Jews of Persia fasted and prayed that they be spared the massacre planned by Haman.

Talmid — student

Talmud — the whole body of Jewish civil and canonical laws and traditions with the commentaries and speculations of the Rabbis, consisting of two parts, the *Mishnah* and *Gemara*

Tamay — spiritually unclean

Tammuz — one of the Hebrew months of the year

Tefillah—(Tefillos) — prayer(s)

Tes — ninth letter of the Hebrew alphabet

Teves — one of the Hebrew months of the year

Tevilah — ritual immersion

Tisha B'Av — Ninth Day of *Av*; an important fast day which marks the destruction of the first Holy Temple in Jerusalem by the Babylonians and also of the second Holy Temple by the Romans.

Torah — Pentateuch; the entire body of traditional Jewish teaching and commandments

Tzaddik (Tzaddikim) — Extremely pious and caring person (people)

Tznius — modesty

Tzom Gedaliah — The Fast of Gedaliah—which commemorates the climax of the disasters that befell the first Jewish Commonwealth, with the murder of the Jewish governor Gedaliah *Ben* Achikam

Vest — the time for a woman's menstrual period

Vov — sixth letter of the Hebrew alphabet

Yiddish(e) — Jewish

Yoledes — a woman who has given birth

Yom Kippur — Day of Atonement—a day of fasting and prayer when we strive to reawaken the latent spiritual power in our souls so that it may become an effective and directing force in our daily conduct

Yom Tov — literally, "good day." The days of the festival during which work was forbidden

Yoreh Deah — the second of the four sections of the *Shulchan Aruch* that deals with a variety of laws, including laws on family purity and dietary laws.

Yud — tenth letter of the Hebrew alphabet

Zocheh — worthy

BIBLIOGRAPHY

This section is not meant to describe the greatness of these *Torah* giants. The information has been provided to give those unfamiliar with a specific personality an idea of when and where he lived.

Aruch Ha-shulchan — See Epstein, Rav Yechiel Michel *Ben* Aharon Yitzchok Halevi.

Ashkenazi, Judah Ben Shimon (18th century) — Born in Frankfort on the Main, Rav Judah seved as a *dayyan* in Tiktin, Poland before 1742. His main work was his commentary on Rav Yosef Karo's *Shulchan Aruch,* the *Be'er Heitev.* The section on *Orach Chaim* was published in Amsterdam in 1742.

Avodas Ha-Kodesh — see Chida, Rav Chaim Yosef Dovid Azulai.

Azulai, Rav Chaim Yosef Dovid — See Chida.

Bachya Ben Asher, Rabbeinu (1255–1340) — A disciple of the Rashbo (Rabbeinu Shlomo *Ben* Aderes 1235–1310). One of the great sages and *Kabbalists* of the 13th century. According to tradition, he lived in Saragossa and served there as a *dayyan* among the *Chachmei Sfard.* Author of many works. Included among them *Rabbeinu Bachya Al Hatorah* written about 1291.

Bais Tefillah — See Papo, Rav Eliezer *Ben* Yitzchak.

Be'er Halacha — See Chofetz Chaim.

Be'er Heitev — See Ashkenazi, Judah Ben Shimon.

Beit Yosef — See Karo, Rav Yosef.

Binas Adam — See Danzig, Rav Avrahom Ben Yechiel Michal.

Chasam Sofer — See Sofer, Rav Moshe.

Chazon Ish — See Karelitz, Rav Avrahom Yeshayahu.

Cheskas Tahara — See Roth, Rav Yechezkel.

Chida—Rav Chaim Yosef Dovid Azulai (1724–1806) — He was a disciple of *Rabbeinu* Chaim *Ben* Attar (Or Ha-Chaim Ha-Kadosh). Born in Yerushalayim, he was known as a *halachist, Kabbalist,* and a bibliographer. Among his famous works are *Birkei Yosef, Shem Ha-Gedolim* and *Sefer Avodas Ha-kodesh* which deals with *tefillos, halacha* and ethics.

Chofetz Chaim—Rav Yisrael Meir Ha-Kohen Kagan (1838–1933) — One of the greatest *tzaddikim* and *Torah* sages of our modern times. At the age of 35 (1873) he published anonymously his first *sefer* in Vilna, *Chofetz Chaim*—("who wants life") which is an intensive study of the laws of *loshon hora* and *r'chilus.* From this sefer he got his name "the Chofetz Chaim." Throughout his life he was a living example of this work. He wrote many of his *sefarim* because he saw there was a need to strengthen some aspect of Torah observance, e.g. *Machne Yisrael, Niddechei Yisrael.* His best known work is the *Mishnah B'rurah,* a six volume masterpiece which comments on *Shulchan Aruch, Orach Chaim.* This work took him 28 years to write. *Mishnah B'rurah* is a necessity in order to understand fully the *Shulchan Aruch* and it is considered authoritative. Also included in this work are the *Sha'ar Hatzion* and the *Be'er Halacha* to further aid in understanding the *Shulchan Aruch.* The Chofetz Chaim was one of the founders of the Agudath Israel, and he helped to organize and set up the "Va'ad Ha-Yeshivot" (Committee on Behalf of Yeshivos) in Europe.

Danzig, Rav Avrahom Ben Yechiel Michal (1748–1820) — Born in Danzig. He studied at a Yeshiva in Prague. Due to his family tradition, he refused to derive any materialistic gain from his studies. Therefore, he earned his living as a merchant. From 1794–1812 he served as a *dayyan* in Vilna. Danzig wrote a number of *halachic* works. He is best known for his *Chayei Adam* with its addendum, the *Nishmas Adam.* This work covered the laws in *Orach Chaim.* He also wrote *Chochmas Adam* with its addendum, the *Binas Adam.* This work covered the laws of *Yoreh Deah.*

Darkei Teshuva — See Shapiro, Rav Tzvi Hirsch.

Eiger, Rav Akiva (1761–1837) — Born in Eisenstadt. He went to study under his uncle Binyamin Wolf Eiger at a very young age when he later became the *Rav* of Posen. There, besides being a brilliant scholar and *halachic* authority, he waged a constant war on the reformers. Among his many works are *Chidushei Rabbi Akiva Eiger, Gilyon HaShas,* and *Shailos Uteshuvos Rabbi Akiva Eiger.* Rav Moshe Sofer (1762–1839), a prominent ancestor of many Torah scholars, was his son-in-law. His son, Shlomo (1786–1852), took his place as Rabbi of Posen upon his death.

Elimelech Ben Elazar, Rav of Lyzhansk (1717–1787). — Rav Elimelech was a disciple of Rav Dov Baer, the *Maggid* of Mezhirech.

After the death of Rav Dov Baer (1772) Rav Elimelech settled in Lyzhansk, Galicia, which as a result became an important *Chassidic* center. His most famous work is *No'am Elimelech.*

Eliyahu Ben Shlomo Avrohom Ha-Kohen, Rav Mai'Izmir (1650–1729) — He was the *dayyan* of Smyrna, and a collector and treasurer over money that was distributed to the poor. Among his over thirty works are *Midrash Talpiyyot* and *Shevet Mussar* (Constantinople 1712). The latter consists of fifty-two chapters, which is the numerical value of his Hebrew name, Eliyahu. These fifty-two chapters are devoted to teaching ethics.

Emden, Rav Yaakov (Ben Tzvi)—Yaavetz (1697–1776) — A disciple of his father Tzvi Hirsch Ashkenazi (Chacham Tzvi). A *Rav, halachic* authority, and *Kabbalist.* Among his famous works is his *Siddur Bais Yaakov,* where he combined grammatical comments and *Kabbalistic* commentary.

Epstein, Rav Yechiel Michel Ben Aharon Yitzchok Halevi (1829–1908) — Born in Bobruisk, Belorussia, he was a *talmid* (student) of Rav Yitzchak of Volozhin. He received *s'micha* from Rav Menachem Mendel of Lubavitch, author of *Tzemach Tzedek.* His main work is the *Aruch Ha-shulchan* based upon the four sections of the *Shulchan Aruch.* He also wrote the *Aruch Ha-shulchan Le-Asid,* (for the future) which deals with the laws that will be pertinent during Messianic times.

Epstein, Rav Yechiel Michel Ben Avrohom Halevi (d. 1706) — *Rav* in Germany, he was most famous for his *Kitzur She'lah,* an abbreviated version of *Sh'nei Luchos Ha-Bris*—She'lah (see She'lah). It also contains new *dinim* and *minhagim* which were taken from the She'lah's works after *Sh'nei Luchos Ha-Bris* was published. He was also author of *Derech Ha-Yoshor Le'Olam Haba,* a siddur with a commentary in Yiddish.

Feinstein, Rav Moshe (1895–1986) —Born in Russia in 1895, Rav Moshe came to New York in 1937, and became the *Rosh Ha-Yeshiva* of Yeshiva Mesivta Tiferes Yerushalayim. He was considered a world renowned leader in Judaism, in *halachic* authority, and was active in many important Jewish Orthodox causes. Among his writings are his *Igros Moshe* which deals with important *halachic* decisions on the four volumes of the *Shulchan Aruch,* and also his *Dibros Moshe* which is a commentary on several volumes of the Talmud.

Ganzfried, Rav Shlomo Ben Yoseph (1804–1886) — Rav Shlomo was born in Ungvar, Hungary, where he also died. Since both of his parents died when he was very young, he was brought up in the home of the local Rabbi, Rav Tzvi Hirsch Heller, one of the outstanding sages of his time. For some time Rav Shlomo served as the head of the *Bais Din* of Ungvar. His most famous work, *Kitzur Shulchan Aruch,* was first published in 1864. Since then many commentaries have been written on this important work, and it has been translated into many languages. This work is based mainly upon the *Shulchan Aruch* of Rav Yosef Karo (1488–1575) and the comments of the R'moh, Rav Moshe Isserles (1520–1572), as well as other previous *halachic* commentaries.

Horowitz, Rav Isaiah Ben Avrohom Ha-Levi — see She'lah.

Igros Moshe — See Feinstein, Rav Moshe.

Kagan, Rav Yisrael Meir Ha-Kohen — see Chofetz Chaim.

Karelitz, Rav Avrahom Yeshayahu (1878–1953) — Born on the 11th of *MarCheshvan* 5639 in Kossova. Known by the title of his profound work entitled *Chazon Ish.* From the time he came to Bnei Brak, *Eretz Yisroel* in 1933, his house became the address where thousands sought advice and guidance. Even though he held no official position, his opinion was sought and respected worldwide.

Karo, Rav Yosef (1488–1575) — Also known as the Beit Yosef which is the title of his brilliant commentary on the Tur (Rav Yaakov ben Asher 1275–1340). Although a noted *Kabbalist* in Tzfat, he is more known as an authority in *halacha.* Among his works are the *Kesef Mishneh,* commentary on the Rambam (1135–1204) and his most famous and important work—the *Shulchan Aruch* (literally a set table). In this work all pertinent Jewish law is brought down in the order following the layout of the Tur. The decisions are based on the opinions of the previous *Chachmei S'fard*. Later on, the Ra'moh's (Rav Moshe Isserles) commentary entitled *Hamapa* (literally, "the tablecloth") was included in all the **Shulchan Aruch**. The Ra'moh represents the opinion of the *Chachmei Ashkenaz*.

Kitzur Sh'nei Luchos Ha-Bris — see Epstein, Rav Yechiel Michel *Ben* Avrohom Halevi.

Kitzur Shulchan Aruch — see Ganzfried, Rav Shlomo *Ben* Yoseph.

Likutei Aitzos — see Nachman of Bratslav, Rav.

Lispchutz, Rav Shabbetai Ben Yaakov Yitzchok (1845–1929) — Rav Shabbetai was born in Rohatyn, Galicia. From 1907 and on, he served as a *Rav* in Bereg-Ilosva (now Russia). He is the author of the *Sefer Segulos Yisroel* and many other works. *Segulos Yisroel* is a compilation of various remedies taken from other original sources.

Maimonides, Rav Moshe Ben Maimon — See Rambam.

Margolios, Rav Chaim Mordechai (d. 1818) — Polish Rabbi. First *Rav* of Brestitzki and later *Rav* of Dubno, where he established a printing office. He was the author of **Shaarei Teshuva**, commentary to the **Shulchan Aruch, Orach Chayim**. It contains extracts from other works, and appears in most editions of the **Shulchan Aruch.**

Minchas Yitzchak — See Weiss, Rav Yitzchak Yaakov.

Mishnah B'rura — see Chofetz Chaim.

Moshe Shemaiah, Rav (17th century) — One of the sages of the 17th century. A son-in-law of Rav Peretz of Lublin. The two known *Sefarim* that he wrote which we possess are **Kodesh La-Hashem** and **Va-Yichtov Moshe.** They both deal with explanations on the *Torah* and on Rashi's (Rav Shlomo Yitzchaki 1040–1105) commentary.

Nachman of Bratslav, Rav (1772–1811) — On his mother's side, he was the great grandson of Yisrael *Ben* Eliezer Ba'al Shem Tov. On his father's side, he was the grandson of Nahman of Gorodenka. The main disciple of Rav Nachman was Nosson *Ben* Naftoli Hertz Sternhartz. He served as his scribe and literary secretary. The first work published was *Likutei Moharan.* Also among his works is *Likutei Aitzos.* This is a gathering of his advice to people in numerous circumstances.

Nachmanides, Rav Moshe Ben Nachman — see Ramban.

Neubart, Rav Yehoshua Yeshaya — Dean of Kollel Beth Medrash Halacha—Moriah in Jerusalem, whose emphasis is clarifying *hilchos Shabbos.* Author of *Shmiras Shabbos Kehilchasa.*

Papo, Rav Eliezer Ben Yitzchak (d. 1824) — Born in Sarajevo, Bosnia, he served as the *Rav* of Silistria, Bulgaria till his death in 1824. Among his works are *Pele Yo-atz, Elef Ha-magen, Chesed La-Alafim* and *Bais Tefillah,* wherein many different *tefillos* for various sitations can be found.

Pardes Rimonim — Novellae on the laws of *niddah.* Written by *Rav Moshe Yitzchak Avigdor,* the head of the *Bais Din* of Shklov. First Published in Vilna in the year 5629.

Rambam—Rav Moshe Ben Maimon—Maimonides (1135–1204) — Born in Cordoba, Spain in the year 1135. A commentator, philosopher, *posek* and royal physician. His main work, the *Yad Hachazaka,* also known as *Mishna Torah* is a monumental *halachic* work containing both opinions of the Babylonian and Jerusalem *Talmuds.* Many commentaries have since been written on this great work. He is also the author of *Moreh Nevuchim* and other important literary works.

Ramban—Rav Moshe Ben Nachman—Nachmanides (1194–1270) — A disciple of Rav Yehuda Bar Yakar. He was one of the *chachmei S'fard,* and the author of very many works covering many different areas of our *Torah* and the *Talmud.* He was also the *Rebbe* of the Rashbo (Rav Shlomo *Ben* Aderes 1235–1310).

Ra'moh (1520–1572) — Acronym for Rav Moshe Isserles—famous *Rav* in Cracow. The personality of Rav Moshe was many faced: a philosopher, *Kabbalist* and most famous for his work *Darkei Moshe,* a commentary of the Tur—(Rav Yaakov Ben Asher 1275–1340) and his commentary *Hamapa* (literally, the tablecloth), which is an addition (הגה) to the *Shulchan Aruch* by the Beit Yosef, (Rav Yosef Karo 1488–1575). The Ra'moh makes comments and additions on the **Shulchan Aruch** which disputes some decisions basing his views on the *Chachmei Ashkenaz* whereas the Beit Yosef bases his opinion on the *Chachmei S'fard.*

Roth, Rav Yechezkel — Born in Temeshvara, Rumania. Arrived in *Eretz Yisroel* as a youngster after World War II. Later appointed *Moreh Tzedek* of Katamon by the Eidah Hacharei-dis of Jerusalem. Emigrated to the United States in 1973. Today he is a *Dayyan* in Boro Park—Brooklyn, New York, and is one of the most noted and outstanding *poskim* of our times. Among his works are **Cheskas Tahara** (on *hilchos niddah*) **Keren HaTorah,** and **Emek HaTeshuva.**

Sefer Chasidim — see Yehuda Ha-Chasid, Rav.

Segulos Yisroel — see Lipschutz, Rav Shabbetai *Ben* Yaakov Yitzchok.

Sha'ar Hatzion — See Chofetz Chaim.

Shaarei Dimah — see Shmuel *Ben* Rav Yehoshua Zelig, Rav Mi'Dalhinov.

Shaarei Teshuvah — See Margolios, Rav Chaim Mordechai.

Shapiro, Rav Tzvi Hirsch (1850–1914) — Rav in Strisov, Poland. After his father's death, he succeeded his father as *Rav* and head of the *Bais Din* in Munkatch. He was one of the foremost fighters against the Reform Movement. Among his works are **Darkei Teshuva** on the **Shulchan Aruch,** and **Be'er Lachay Ro'ee** on the **Zohar.**

She'lah Ha-kadosh—Rav Isaiah Ben Avrohom Ha-Levi Horowitz (1565?–1630) — Born in Prague. He was a disciple of the Maharshal (Rav Shlomo Luria 1510–1573), and also of the R'moh (Rav Moshe Isserles 1520–1572). A *Rav* in the cities of Frankfurt, Vienna, Cracow, Posen. He was an authority on *halacha*, and a renowned *Kabbalist*. He was the author of many works. Among them, his most prominent work, **Sh'nei Luchos Ha-Bris,** known as **The She'Lah,** first printed in Amsterdam in 1649. In this work, *halacha, kabbalah* and various *tefillos* are combined to give the reader a guide for an ethical life.

Shevet Mussar — see Eliyahu *Ben* Shlomo Avrohom Ha-Kohen, Rav Mai'Izir.

Shmiras Shabbos Kehilchasa — See Neubart, Rav Yehoshua Yeshaya.

Shmuel Ben Rav Yehoshua Zelig, Rav Mi'Dalhinov (d. 1858) — He served as a *Rav* in Dalhinov and Eliyah. He is also known as Shmuel *Ha-Koton*. Rav Shmuel died on the third day of the month of Av 5618 (1858). Among his works are **Minchas Shmuel** and **Shaarei Dimah**. *Shaarei Dimah* consists of many *tefillos,* said at several holy places and on various important occasions.

Siddur Bais Yaakov — see Emden, Rav Yaakov (Ben Tzvi).

Sidrei Taharah — Novellae on *hilchos niddah* and *tevilah.* Written by **Rav Elchanan Ben Rav Shmuel Zanvil.** First published in Berlin in the year 5543.

Sofer, Moshe; Chasam Sofer (1762–1839) — Born in Frankfurt. Was a loyal student of Rav Nossen Adler (1741–1800). In the year 1806, he was appointed *Rav* of Pressburg, Hungary, where he remained for the rest of his life. During his stay in Pressburg, he founded his Yeshiva, the largest Yeshiva since the time of the Babylonian *Talmud.* After his first wife died in 1812, he married the daughter of Rav Akiva Eiger (1761–1837), one of the greatest scholars of his time. Among his many works is the **Chasam Sofer,** which is a brilliant work on the *Talmud,* commentaries on the *Torah* and sermons, and his **Shailos Uteshuvos Chasam Sofer** which deals with halachic discussion. These works were all published by his family after his death.

Sperling, Rav Avraham Yitzchok (5611–5681) — Rav Avraham was born in Levov, and spent many years investigating the reasons for Jewish customs. Originally he was going to include some of his findings in the **Siddur Safah B'rurah,** but instead, in 5651, he decided to print a separate *sefer,* **Taamei Ha-minhagim U'mekorai Ha-dinim,** wherein one can find explanations for many Jewish laws and customs.

Taamei Ha-minhagim U'mekorai Ha-dinim — see Sperling, Rav Avraham Yitzchok.

Taz—Turei Zahav—Segal, Rav David (1586–1667) — Lived in Poland. *Talmid* of his father-in-law the Bach, Rav Yoel Sirkis (1561–1640). Giant in Torah study. Served different communities as *Rav* and head of the *Bais Din*. Best known for his widely accepted *Taz*, **acronym for** *Turei Zahav*, title by which he began to be called. In his *Turei Zahav* on the 4 parts of the *Shulchan Aruch*, he places the original source beside each *halacha* and the views of the later *Poskim* and establishes the final *halacha* clearly.

Techina Kol Bo HaChodosh — A book of prayers written in Yiddish containing prayers for all occasions. The copyright is held by Rabbi Meshulam Greenfield of Ateres Bookbinding Company, 60 Broadway, Brooklyn, New York 11211.

Va-Yictov Moshe — see Moshe Shemaiah, Rav.

Weiss, Rav Yitzchak Yaakov — Formerly *Dayyan* of Manchester, England. Emigrated to *Eretz Yisroel*. Appointed Head of the *Bais Din* of the Eidah Hachareidis of Jerusalem. One of the foremost *poskim* of our time. Author of *Minchas Yitzchak*.

Yehuda Ha-Chasid, Rav Yehuda Ben Shmuel (1150–1217). A disciple of Rav Yaakov *Ben* Eliezer Ha-m'kubal. One of the most prominent scholars of the Middle Ages among the *chachmei Ashkenaz*, in the fields of ethics and theology. Author of *Sefer Chasidim, Za-va'at Rav Yehuda Ha-Chasid* (The Will of Rav Yehuda the Pious), and many other works. His famous *Sefer Chasidim* deals with both ethical and *halachic* matters. His own sage advice is blended in as well.